# BASIC INCOME

'Basic income is an ethical imperative, and a matter of common justice, freedom and basic security. In our age of uncertainty, this book shows it is also a matter of mental and physical health.'
**Guy Standing, author of *Basic Income: And How We Can Make It Happen***

'This accessible and clearly written book brings an original public health lens to the case for a basic income.'
**Baroness Ruth Lister of Burtersett**

'Just as it was once thought impossible that we would pay unemployment benefit to those without work, so too many cannot imagine the implementation of basic income. You don't need to be in that group: read this book!'
**Danny Dorling, University of Oxford**

'This book is a real achievement: using astute modelling and pathbreaking arguments around health and economy, the authors make the clearest case yet for a basic income. If you are a sceptic or an advocate, you need to read this.'
**Will Stronge, The Autonomy Institute**

'This is a wise little book on the prospects of basic income in the UK. It shows that we would be much better off introducing a robust income floor now than picking up the pieces once people are already hurt and ill from the consequences of income poverty. It frames basic income as a public health measure and shows how it can help us build healthier communities.'
**Juliana Bidadanure, New York University School of Law**

'Universal Basic Income: a common sense policy and a common sense exploration of how transformational it would be for society.'
**Dave Beck, University of Salford**

# BASIC INCOME
## The Policy That Changes Everything

Matthew Johnson, Kate Pickett, Daniel Nettle,
Howard Reed, Elliott Johnson and Ian Robson

First published in Great Britain in 2025 by

Policy Press, an imprint of
Bristol University Press
University of Bristol
1–9 Old Park Hill
Bristol
BS2 8BB
UK
+44 (0)117 374 6645
bup-info@bristol.ac.uk

Details of international sales and distribution partners are available at
policy.bristoluniversitypress.co.uk

© Bristol University Press 2025

British Library Cataloguing in Publication Data
A catalogue record for this book is available from the British Library

ISBN 978-1-4473-7400-8 paperback
ISBN 978-1-4473-7401-5 ePub
ISBN 978-1-4473-7402-2 ePdf

The right of Matthew Johnson, Kate Pickett, Daniel Nettle, Howard Reed, Elliott Johnson and Ian Robson to be identified as authors of this work has been asserted by them in accordance with the Copyright, Designs and Patents Act 1988.

All rights reserved: no part of this publication may be reproduced, stored in a retrieval system, or transmitted in any form or by any means, electronic, mechanical, photocopying, recording, or otherwise without the prior permission of Bristol University Press.

Every reasonable effort has been made to obtain permission to reproduce copyrighted material. If, however, anyone knows of an oversight, please contact the publisher.

The statements and opinions contained within this publication are solely those of the author and not of the University of Bristol or Bristol University Press. The University of Bristol and Bristol University Press disclaim responsibility for any injury to persons or property resulting from any material published in this publication.

Bristol University Press and Policy Press work to counter discrimination on grounds of gender, race, disability, age and sexuality.

Cover design: Keenan Design

Bristol University Press and Policy Press use environmentally responsible print partners.

# Contents

| | |
|---|---|
| List of figures and tables | vi |
| About the authors | vii |
| Acknowledgements | ix |
| Introduction | 1 |
| 1  Why basic income? | 8 |
| 2  Securing the basics: reducing poverty | 29 |
| 3  Freedom from stress | 40 |
| 4  Changing behaviour and strengthening communities | 52 |
| 5  Care across generations | 65 |
| 6  A collective return on investment | 76 |
| 7  If you like basic income, you're in the majority | 88 |
| Conclusion | 110 |
| Notes | 114 |
| Index | 133 |

# List of figures and tables

## Figures
| | | |
|---|---|---|
| 1.1 | The overall logic of our case for basic income, showing how the policy has positive effects identifiable at several different levels, via several different pathways | 15 |
| 7.1 | Distribution of support for basic income, on a 0–100 scale, in the Red Wall survey, broken down by age group (A), homeownership (B) and 2019 general election vote (C) | 94 |
| 7.2 | Visualisation of trade-off between personal income tax rates and poverty, separated by Labour (left) and Conservative (right) voting in 2019 | 97 |

## Tables
| | | |
|---|---|---|
| 1.1 | Summary of basic income payments under the three proposed schemes | 13 |
| 2.1 | Percentage changes in household income compared to the status quo, for each of the basic income schemes | 32 |

## About the authors

**The Common Sense Policy Group** comprises academics, policy makers, third sector leaders, community representatives, media figures and people with lived experience. The Chair of the Common Sense Policy Group is Matthew Johnson. We are all committed to creating a fair, equal and inclusive Britain through developing and influencing policies to address inequality and exclusion. We aim to present feasible, affordable and popular evidence-based policies that can form the basis of a programme for progressive government.

**Elliott Johnson** is Vice-Chancellor's Fellow in Public Policy at Northumbria University. His research currently focuses on basic income, in particular, understanding its health impact, economic feasibility, public acceptability and the development of narratives capable of persuading opponents.

**Matthew Johnson** is Chair of the Common Sense Policy Group and Professor of Public Policy at Northumbria University. His work focuses on the relationship between financial insecurity, health, public opinion and means of persuading people to vote in their own interests.

**Daniel Nettle** is Professor of Community Wellbeing at Northumbria University and a CNRS researcher in the Evolution and Social Cognition team at Institut Jean Nicod, Paris. His work focuses on the relationship between poverty, inequality and behaviour and in developing public policy to improve outcomes.

**Kate Pickett** is Professor of Epidemiology at the University of York and co-author with Richard Wilkinson of *The Spirit Level* and *Inner Level*. She is co-founder of the Equality Trust and has pioneered understanding of the impacts of poverty and inequality as social determinants of health.

**Howard Reed** is Senior Research Fellow in Public Policy at Northumbria University and Director of Landman Economics. He is former Chief Economist at IPPR and a leading international expert in economic microsimulation. He leads the Common Sense Policy Group's costing, affordability and tax-benefit analysis.

**Ian Robson** is Assistant Professor in Social Work, Education and Community Wellbeing at Northumbria University. He is a methodological innovator who enables new knowledge and practice change in the fields of collaborative enquiry, social design and inclusion of marginalised groups.

## Acknowledgements

This book is based on the results of a long-term programme of peer-reviewed and published work that has included a large number of collaborators. We appreciate, deeply, their collegiality and the unique insights they have contributed to this work. Thanks in particular to: Melissa Bateson, Coralie Chevallier, Joe Chrisp, Jonathan Coates, Jamie Cooke, Richard Cookson, Anne Corrigan, Benoît de Courson, Dan Degerman, Rocco Friebel, Robert Geyer, Cleopatra Goodman, Julia Hines, Neil Howard, Chris Kypridemos, Stewart Lansley, Alice Mathers, James Morrison, Martin O'Flaherty, Fiorella Parra Mujica, Gillian Pepper, Matt Smith, Graham Stark, Lena Swedlow, Riley Thorold, Aase Villadsen and Hannah Webster.

The underpinning research for this book was in part funded by The Wellcome Trust and The National Institute for Health and Social Care Research. Kate Pickett acknowledges funding from the UK Prevention Research Partnership collaboration, ActEarly. Daniel Nettle acknowledges funding from the Centre Nationale de la Recherche Scientifique and the Agence Nationale de la Recherche.

## Introduction

This is a small book about a big idea. The idea is a simple one that solves complex problems. The idea is that the government should pay each of the residents of the country a *basic income*, funded through taxation. A basic income is a weekly cash payment, made to individuals not households, which they receive as of right, automatically, and which cannot be taken away.

The level of basic income could initially be quite modest, but it should be increased over time as the wealth and wellbeing of society increases. Basic income will not replace earned income: the funding model we propose assumes, indeed requires, that people will still seek paid activities in the labour market. There is every reason to think that they will, because they want their lives to be more than basic in ways that matter to them. For most people, meaningful paid work and material affluence are central to achieving this. The point of the basic income is not to replace an open economy, but to enhance it. Specifically, the point is to put a sound floor under everyone's feet. This floor will make our lives more predictable, avoid the prospect of the worst kinds of outcomes, and allow us to take on the things we are good at and want to do, rather than feeling forced into making choices that are bad for us, go against our better judgement and make us unwell. Knowing that such a floor is in place will make people freer, more prosocial and more productive. Of particular importance, it will make them healthier. The benefit will flow most immediately to those of us with the lowest and most precarious incomes, but in the long run everyone will benefit, due to the knock-on impacts on health, productivity, crime, families and community life. This is our contention, and we will try to persuade you that it is a plausible one.

The goal of putting a floor under everyone's feet, so that the very worst possibilities of poverty, hunger and destitution can be avoided, is widely shared. For this reason, countries already have a patchwork of mechanisms designed to fulfil this goal in various ways. In the United Kingdom (UK), we have Universal Credit, Personal Independence Payment, Child Benefit, the state pension, the personal income tax allowance, the minimum wage, and so on. We argue that this patchwork is a less effective and efficient way than basic income of achieving the right goal: a floor for everyone to stand on. This is why basic income should be introduced.

The other mechanisms are less good because they are outdated, complex, difficult and sometimes humiliating to navigate and receive. They also have all kinds of perverse incentives baked into their design. To maintain the limited and often inadequate conditional payments that the current system provides, there are incentives to stay sick rather than getting well; to be inactive rather than do things that are personally and socially useful; and to turn down paid but insecure work. Above all, the current mechanisms fail because they miss the point. The point of the social safety net is to give people the *security* of knowing that their lives are, in key ways, *predictable*, so that they can make good decisions and live healthily. A patchwork of conditional, after-the-fact transfers for which we need to apply, not knowing whether we will be successful, which take an uncertain time to adjudicate, and can be withdrawn at any time, does not do this job well enough. It is like having parachutes available, but asking us to apply online for one in the event we find ourselves to have fallen out of an aeroplane.

It would be better if people went through their lives with their parachutes already on. Having such a measure of security and protection would produce a social and economic transformation, disproportionate in its depth and breadth to the cost of running the scheme. This is why we describe basic income as the policy that changes everything.

There have been many books and pamphlets on basic income already, including overviews by Guy Standing[1] and Philippe van Parijs and Yannick Vanderborght.[2] The argument for a basic income goes back at least to the 19th century, and arguably to the 18th. Notably, the arguments for basic income come from a number of different political quarters: libertarians wanting to simplify the state; liberals wanting to increase freedom; socialists wanting to spread resources to the many not just the few; greens wanting to move away from the pursuit of ever-greater material production and consumption. The grounds of their cases for basic income are very varied. There is the case to be made on fundamental ethical grounds: the legacies of the land and the ingenuity of the people who went before us belong to the whole of society, so we should all get our common share. There is the case that can be made in terms of the consequences for society: in a good society, people would be free from domination, either by the state, by their employers or by one another. Basic income is not dissimilar to Virginia Woolf's prerequisite for writing: a lock on one's door and £500 a year (actually, £500 a year was quite a lot of money when Woolf wrote that; the basic income schemes we will propose amount to something rather more modest). The security provided by basic income enables us to do the valuable things we need to do.

Another case is based on the benefits for economic productivity once perverse incentives are reduced and poverty traps eliminated. Still another sees basic income as providing a handy tool for ensuring economic resilience in the event of recessions, or crises like the COVID-19 pandemic. Some cases are prudential: it's really bad to have people around who are destitute, desperate and hungry, not just for those individuals but, obviously, for everyone else too. A basic income helps ensure that rarely happens. Some cases are administrative: it has just become too hard and expensive for the state to track everyone's changing financial circumstances well enough to work out what they should receive under conditional schemes, and basic income is administratively simpler.

We are sympathetic to all these well-rehearsed cases, but we will not review them in full. The emphasis of our book is somewhat different. Our case is a pragmatic one, concerned with consequences.[3] For many years, we have been concerned by the fact that, despite Britain's unprecedented total amount of wealth, so many of us are unwell, physically and mentally. We have concluded that we will never be able to deal with this public health crisis just by trying to provide people with medical care once they are already sick. We need to go further 'upstream', to the causes of our sickness, and the causes of those causes, and make preventative interventions there. The causes of the causes have a lot to do, directly and indirectly, with the distribution of material resources: absolute and relative levels of access to those resources, and the predictability of access to them. Guaranteeing a predictable minimum of material resources to everyone is the mother of all health interventions. Thus, this book has a distinctive focus on the argument for basic income from public health. Health is something everyone should agree is desirable; and ill health is astonishingly costly in terms of lost economic activity, as well as the costs of treating it.

As well as being health-focused, this book is fundamentally pragmatic and practical in its treatment of the topic. It is pragmatic because we are less interested in whether, in a thought experiment about an ideal society, there would be something like a basic income, important though it is to think about these fundamental questions. We do not view abstract rights as being valuable in and of themselves independently of the consequences they produce. Rather, we are interested in what good basic income would do for us, and whether it would be implementable given where we are as a society right now. This raises all kinds of detailed questions: how much should the basic income be? How would it interact with institutions we already have like the benefit and income tax systems? What savings might it lead to? Would it be affordable? Would there be political support for it across a broad-enough coalition to get it adopted?

Because the answers to these questions depend in detail on the existing social and economic situation, we take the UK as our context and case study throughout the book. We give a lot of figures relevant to the UK in 2025. We are aware that these figures will date, but the larger point in service of which we cite them is often more enduring. The UK is not the only country that needs basic income. Indeed, there are policy proposals and pilots underway and under development on several continents, and in a wide variety of contexts. Though these are exciting developments, we will not review them here. We think it is important to ground our arguments in the detail and particulars of one country at one point in time. Our goal here is to show that, for the UK in 2025, the path to a basic income, via a starter scheme, is administratively, economically and politically a lot more straightforward and feasible than you might think.

And if that is true of the UK in 2025, it will be true at later dates, and in other countries, as well. Only the particulars will need adapting.

The book is practical in that we are interested in what concrete difference basic income would make to our lives. We mean the lives of everyone, throughout the UK, but we are particularly influenced by our experience living and working in areas of Northern England. Particular contexts we have worked in include Newcastle upon Tyne; Jarrow, South Tyneside; Ashington and Blyth, Northumberland; and Bradford, West Yorkshire. These are all communities sometimes, perhaps unfortunately, described as 'left behind'. Formerly industrial, over many decades they have seen a gradual loss of their main economic bases. Today they are among the poorest places in the UK, and among the least healthy. In all these places, we have worked with community partners: in Newcastle, with the city council and Children and Families Newcastle; in Jarrow, with a community organisation called Big Local Jarrow; in Blyth, with Northumberland County Council; in Bradford, with the Born in Bradford[4] and ActEarly[5] research programmes, which aim to improve the health of children.

We have carried out surveys and interviews, focus groups and community meetings.[6] We have spoken to people of all ages, with a particular emphasis on the younger age group. By engaging in this way, we were trying to understand how community members experience their current social and economic lives. Perhaps more importantly, we were trying to understand their thoughts about how the state could make their lives better. Do they see basic income as having the same transformative potential that we see it as having? Can they anticipate downsides or problems that we have failed to spot? Is the policy comprehensible and appealing to most people? We will be weaving insights from the community engagement into the book in two ways. Sometimes we draw upon it in the main text, at points where those conversations are relevant to the argument. In addition, we end each of the main chapters with a brief case study, usually from one of the community contexts, to make the argument of the chapter more concrete, and relate it to everyday life.

In what follows, Chapter 1 presents our central argument for why basic income is a good idea, both in general, and specifically for the UK context and the current time. We present our policy proposal for the UK, and a simple schematic map of its positive impacts. We trace these from the level of improved individual lives, through to that of aggregate societal changes such as reduced healthcare expenditure, lower crime, higher productivity, stronger communities and more entrepreneurship. These changes, in turn, provide savings and new sources of income for the government that would offset the scheme's cost. The later chapters of the book essentially work through the different pathways that make up this schematic map.

Chapter 2 shows how basic income, despite the breadth of its coverage, is a very effective and targeted way of reducing poverty. Chapter 3 turns to the effect of basic income on stress. We isolate uncertainty as the central feature of our current precarious economy, link uncertainty to stress, and examine the impact of basic income on both. Importantly, we argue that because basic income reduces uncertainty, it can improve the wellbeing even of the people whose net incomes do not increase (because the gain of their basic income will be clawed back in higher taxes). In Chapter 4, we discuss the idea of the double dividend: once our world has become safer and more predictable, we will respond with behavioural changes that amplify this effect, and make us better off still. We will become more long-termist, more motivated to look after ourselves and our environments and more socially oriented. This dividend will produce both personal and community-wide benefits.

Chapter 5 examines the impact of basic income on the provision of care. Basic income gives people the support needed to devote parts of their energy to caring responsibilities – such as for children or older relatives – if they wish, and the flexibility to move seamlessly between paid work and the work of caring. This produces benefits for those giving care, and to the children, older people and people with disabilities who receive it. In so doing it provides a saving to the state, and a good to society at large. Chapter 6 zooms out and tries to characterise the collective transformation basic income could bring at the level of British society as a whole: how would it change class, community and relationships, and how can it help reverse the loss of authority and dignity that so many people have felt in recent decades?

## Introduction

In view of all the potential benefits we will set out, you might wonder why basic income is not in the manifestoes of any of the largest political parties. There are numerous reasons for this. Some are to do with lag and inertia: alternative institutions to basic income were more viable in previous time periods, and political parties are having trouble catching up. Some of the reasons have to do with sectional interests being opposed to one or other feature of basic income for different reasons. But the myth that there would be no support for the introduction of a basic income in the UK is just that: a myth. Drawing on our own polling and research, in Chapter 7 we show that support for the policy is already extremely high and broadly based. Moreover, the concerns that people do have are amenable to effective argumentation. In short, a lack of public appetite is not the reason basic income is not already happening. We present the case that basic income would be popular as well as effective and feasible.

# 1
# Why basic income?

Making an automatic payment to everyone in the country, every week, for ever, seems like rather an extreme move. Many people are getting by or even doing well financially as it is. If the problem is that some people's incomes are too low, why make payments to everyone else? How big would the payments be? What has the average Briton done to deserve them? And how can the government possibly afford to do it? These are all good questions. This chapter presents the basic income policy we have in mind, and explains why we think it is a good reform for our time. Its arguments will be further unpacked in the chapters that follow.

The effects of basic income are better targeted than they seem: they specifically address the problems that most afflict us now, and they most help the people who are most in need. Introducing basic income thus has clear advantages over alternative reforms like improving the existing welfare system. The positive consequences of introducing basic income are multiple, and plausibly extremely large. Many of them, in addition to being good for their own sakes, will feed money back into the Treasury. For example, economic productivity and dynamism will increase, health will improve, and we will spend less on trying to fix social problems. This makes the net cost of the transition to basic income less than the upfront expenditures imply. Before we plunge into presenting and justifying our scheme, though, it is necessary to set out why we think *any* reform of our social institutions is necessary. What is wrong with things as they are?

## What are the problems that need to be solved?

In 1980, life expectancy in the UK was 77 years for women and 71 years for men. In 2022, it was 83 for women and 79 for men.[1] The median household disposable income, adjusted for family size, was equivalent to £16,227 in 1980, whereas in 2022 it was £32,349.[2] This represents a doubling. So, people in Britain have longer lives now than 40 years ago, during which they will be richer. Doesn't this sound like a success story?

Certainly, the residents of Britain don't seem to feel that way. In 2023, 76 per cent of people polled felt Britain was becoming a worse place to live, against 6 per cent who felt it was getting better.[3] In 2019 (before the COVID-19 pandemic and 2023 cost of living crisis), fewer than 20 per cent were prepared to predict that the country's best years lay ahead, and only 36 per cent thought it likely that today's young people would have better lives than their parents.[4] In the computerised notes that British family doctors take when people come to see them, the incidence of selecting a code related to anxiety increased by 60 per cent between 2003 and 2018.[5] The upward trend was restricted to those younger than 55, and sharpest in those under 25.[6] In population snapshots, the proportion of working adults meeting the clinical criteria for a common mental disorder – basically, chronic worry, sadness, hopelessness or agitation – was estimated at 14 per cent in 1993, but 18 per cent in 2014. A 2023 update is in progress, and may show a further increase.[7] Again, the young suffer the most.

Our lives have not become longer by as much as we might have hoped, and certainly not healthier. Overall life expectancy, after its earlier upward climb, has made essentially zero progress since 2011.[8] Healthy life expectancy, which is the number of years you can expect to be both alive and in good or excellent health, actually went backwards over this time period. For England as a whole, it went from 63 years and two months to 62 years and four months for men; and from 63 years and ten months to 62 years and eight months for women.[9] The state pension age is currently 67, meaning that many of us cannot anticipate any healthy retirement at all. Some regions fared much worse than the average. The UK government's Levelling Up White Paper highlighted differences of up to 18 years lived in good health between the most and least deprived areas of Britain.[10] The loss in the last decade has been greatest away from London: 20 months for men in Northeast England and 31 months for women in the East Midlands.

Ill health is a cost, and avoidable ill health is a particularly cruel one. It costs time that could be spent with family. It costs opportunities to contribute to the community. It eats into our energy for pursuing the lives that we regard as good and worthwhile, whatever they may be. It has monetary costs for society too. By summer 2022, 2.5 million people of working age were economically inactive for health reasons, up from less than two million people five years earlier.[11] The increase has, again, been greatest among the young. The UK government expects to spend £61 billion in 2023/2024 supporting people of working age who are ill or disabled.[12] This is around half of all the social security budget that is not spent on retirement pensions.[13]

The most prevalent types of ill health are the common mental disorders, such as depression and anxiety, which are incontrovertibly related to stress. After these come conditions that are classified as physical, but in which stress is known to play a role, either in making the conditions more likely to begin, slower to heal, or more severe than they otherwise would be: chronic pain, diabetes and metabolic problems, cardiovascular disease. We also know that both ill health and stress are related to access to material resources, both directly and indirectly through the hassles, powerlessness, compromises and indignities to which material want exposes people.[14]

It was not supposed to be like this. One hundred years ago, John Maynard Keynes projected that by now 'the economic problem' of material scarcity would have been solved.[15] His main preoccupation was how we would find purpose in a world where making ends meet would not be our most pressing objective anymore. Fifty years later, the architects of the neoliberal settlement, the Thatcherites in the UK, were confident that rolling back and privatising the state would produce such a wave of economic dynamism that abundance, and consequent wellbeing, would trickle down to all. They envisaged a future in which state provision of services and cash benefits would simply wither away because people would not need such support any more. Essentially everyone would be wealthy and independent enough able to seek the goods and services they wanted through the marketplace, without the need for government intervention other than to enforce contracts and ensure market competition.

Needless to say, these projections have not come true. Despite decades of (uneven) growth, the utopian vision of broadly spread abundance has not been reached. Around one-fifth of adults in the UK currently find it fairly or very difficult to make ends meet each month,[16] and that is with the lifestyle they have, not the lifestyle they would want. In January 2024, one estimate was that over eight million adults (15 per cent of households) were food insecure, meaning they went a day without eating, or ate less, because they couldn't access or afford food.[17]

The overall size of the economic pie has grown, at least according to standard measures, but a greater and greater share has been captured by the owners of wealth and those on the highest incomes.[18] Foundational liveability – the practical capability for most people to thrive and pursue their purposes in the places where they spend their time – has reduced for most of us.[19] The promise of the neoliberal settlement has not been made good. As anthropologist and activist David Graeber asked: where are the flying cars?[20]

When you don't deliver on promises, you are not trusted. Not surprisingly, fewer than two in ten UK adults say they trust the government, and only three in ten feel they have any say in what the government does.[21] Without wanting to be alarmist, this is not a sustainable situation. Political institutions persist when they provide enough people with the social basis of respect – which includes feeling heard – and the capabilities to live lives they find satisfactory. When a sufficiently large number of people feel that their absolute and relative positions are declining – what the anthropologist Peter Turchin calls *popular immiseration* – social upheaval is likely unless the governing institutions can respond creatively through reform.[22] We have seen this upheaval surfacing in the recent unpredictability of votes and the rise of populist parties.

None of the assertions we have made in this section are disputed, or based on hidden information that only we have.

The numbers we have quoted all come from the government itself, and other reputable surveys accessible to anyone with an internet connection. In Jarrow, two things became immediately apparent in our focus groups. These seemed to be shared, obvious truths rather than outlying or even debatable opinions. The first was that 'poverty is everything' in Jarrow and communities like it – scarcity of resources defines people's lived experience.[23] People knew from their own experience what the statistics were telling us.

The second was that the current welfare system is characterised by general inefficiency, ineffectiveness and indignity. As one participant said, to general agreement in his group, 'It's not like they're helping you. They're not giving you the help that you need.' Another added: 'They're just on your back, pushing you towards menial jobs, low-paid, crap, shitty work that this government obviously would like to see everybody in – low-paid, underpaid work, where you cannot actually buy food, so you go into food banks as well.'

So, the facts are known to policy makers and citizens alike. Yet, oddly and myopically, mainstream political parties offer weaker and weaker reforms as the need for reform becomes more and more urgent. Like homeopaths, they seem to believe in remedies that have been diluted to the point where they carry only the memory of hope.

## Our basic income scheme proposals

This book is about basic income in general, but our research and thinking centre around three specific basic income policy proposals that we have developed and modelled for the UK. These are imaginatively named scheme 1, scheme 2 and scheme 3. The weekly payments under each scheme are shown in Table 1.1. Every permanent UK resident would receive a weekly payment, according to their age group, as shown in the table.

The schemes were designed with somewhat different purposes. Scheme 1 is something that could be introduced straight away. It gives every adult £75 a week, every child £50 a week to replace Child Benefit, and pensioners something close to the current state pension. We envisage it being introduced alongside some

Table 1.1: Summary of basic income payments under the three proposed schemes

| Weekly payment | Scheme 1 | Scheme 2 | Scheme 3 |
| --- | --- | --- | --- |
| Child under 18 | £50 | £75 | £100 |
| Adult under 65 | £75 | £185 | £295 |
| Adult 65+ | £205 | £205 | £295 |

fairly simple changes to the tax code: abolition of the personal allowances for income tax and National Insurance, equalisation of National Insurance for the employed and self-employed, and three percentage points addition to the rates of personal income tax. Coupled with these changes, scheme 1 would be fiscally neutral straight away. This means that government expenditure the year after the scheme's introduction would be no higher than the year before. As we will argue later, in the medium term we think government expenditure would go down, through savings to the National Health Service (NHS) and personal social services. It is fiscal neutrality that means our schemes would not cause inflation. The government is not simply printing money, but increasing its receipts and reducing other expenditures to balance the outlay.

Scheme 3 sets the basic income payments equal to what has been called the Minimum Income Standard (MIS). MIS has been worked out by economists in consultation with the public, and is supposed to represent the amount of income currently required in order for a UK household to have an acceptable standard of living. If we set the basic income at the MIS, then by construction, there should be no one in the UK unable to have an acceptable standard of living. This is a much more ambitious goal than scheme 1, and funding it would require more fundamental fiscal changes for fiscal neutrality. As well as higher rates of personal income tax, these might include wealth taxes, and forms of carbon tax. We see scheme 3 as an aspiration that government could move towards, progressively making the tax changes and reaping the expenditure savings of the smaller schemes along the way, over the timescale of perhaps a decade. Scheme 2 is a halfway house, whose introduction could be envisaged say five years after scheme 1.

## How would basic income solve our problems?

The thesis of this book is that basic income schemes like those just described are the best way of addressing the problems and malaise described at the beginning of the chapter. This puts the burden on us to say why we think basic income would do so much good. First, though, a brief note on terminology. We prefer the name *basic income* to *universal basic income*, which you will encounter describing the same idea. No one thinks basic income should be *completely* universal. There would be conditions of legitimate entitlement, just as there are for the vote. To receive it, you would need to be a legal permanent resident of the country who, if not born here, has served a period of qualification. We might consider withholding payments from people convicted of a crime and given a custodial sentence. We will often contrast basic income with existing *conditional* welfare payments. Current welfare payments can be conditional in several different senses. They may have behavioural conditions, like the requirement to look for work; financial conditions, like not earning more than a certain threshold (aka means testing); medical conditions, like an assessment of illness; or contributory conditions, meaning that people can only take out to the extent they have previously paid in. We use the same term – conditional – to capture all and any of these senses. The point of difference of basic income is that it is not conditional in any of these ways, only on being a legitimate and qualifying legal resident.

Basic income changes everything because it improves health, understood at several different *levels*, through several different *pathways*. Figure 1.1 summarises the way we think about it working. The levels are grouped horizontally, and the pathways are the top-to-bottom sets of arrows.

In the top half of the diagram, we see how the effects of the policy filter through to individual brains, hearts, backs and abdomens to produce better individual health states. We have known for a long time now that although health states play out within the body, they are strongly affected by influences coming from society. That is, we are likely to end up in worse health states when we suffer severe material want, when we lack autonomy and control, and when our livelihoods are volatile and

## Why basic income?

**Figure 1.1:** The overall logic of our case for basic income, showing how the policy has positive effects identifiable at several different levels, via several different pathways

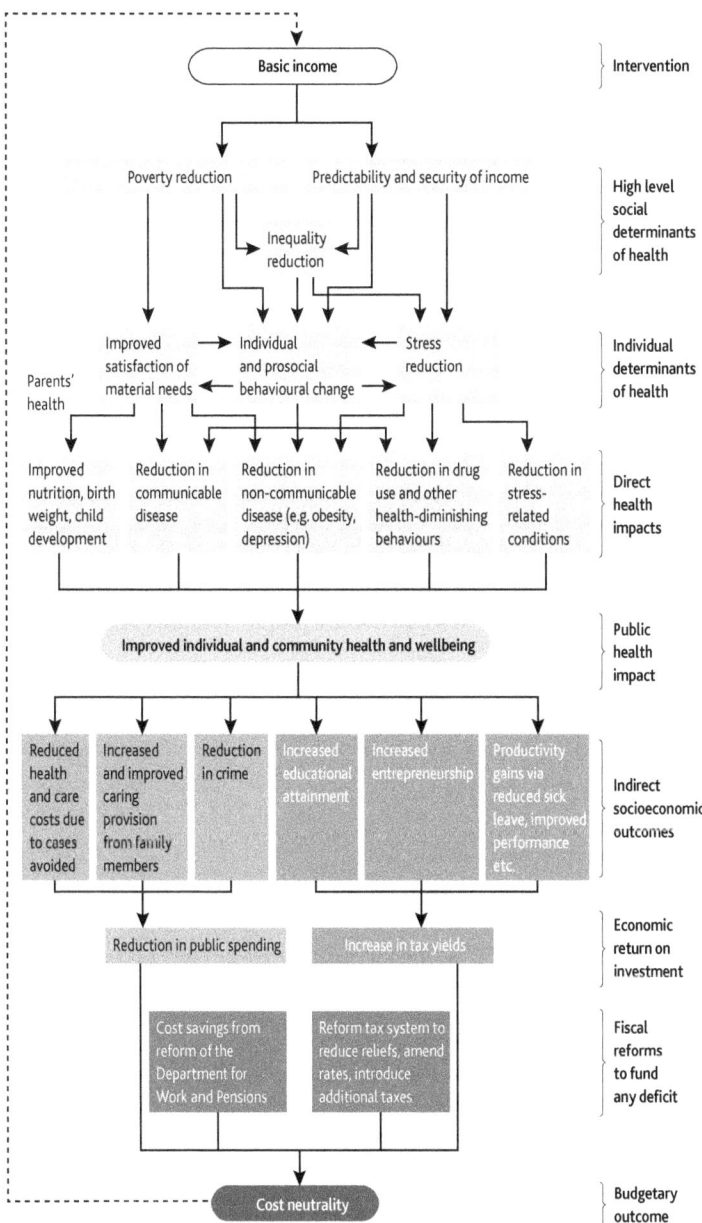

Source: Adapted from M.T. Johnson, E.A. Johnson, K.E. Pickett and D. Nettle, 'Designing Trials of Universal Basic Income for Health Impact', *Journal of Public Health* 44 (2021): 408–416.

unpredictable. These personal determinants flow from society-level economic parameters like the rate of extreme poverty, the inequality of income and wealth, and the degree of security and unpredictability in people's means of subsistence. In a nutshell, when policy makers intervene at the macro scale on the rate of poverty, the inequality of the distribution of resources, and the degree of certainty and predictability in subsistence, they necessarily have a downstream effect on individuals' material want, insecurity and capacity to exert control.[24] These individual states, in turn, have effects on our brains and bodies that are as real as those of drugs or poisons.

The mid-point of the diagram, then, is a distribution of individual health states where more people are well and fewer are sick. The macro-scale reform at the top has flowed through to more individual people feeling well and able as well as, we will argue in what follows, being in a meaningful sense more free. The bottom half of the diagram shows how this better distribution of health states flows through to the 'health' of society and the public finances. Healthcare costs, as well as the costs of supporting people on sick leave, go down. Care of families and children gets better on average. The crime rate goes down. People are more productive and undertake new economic ventures. People are in situations that allow them to be better citizens.

These consequences are in themselves justification enough for the reform. But, since people are bound to ask about financial sustainability, these consequences are also good news for the Treasury. The 'health' of the government's balance sheet improves through reductions in expenditure and increases in tax yields. Coupled with reforms to the tax code and the benefits system that are more than justified by the fact that everyone will receive a basic income, this means that the government's operating deficit would need to be no larger than it is now, and the amount of money available for schools, defence and so forth would not be reduced.

In addition to dividing the diagram into horizontal parts, we can also trace the parallel vertical routes through it. In particular, we see basic income as having a positive effect on health states via three different causal pathways. Though in practice these are bound up with and compound one another, they are conceptually distinct.

First, basic income is an effective way of reducing poverty. Those of us with the highest unmet material need get those needs met more effectively. The evidence that poverty and material need have powerful effects on health, even within high income countries, is now incontrovertible.[25] So, the reduction of this need is the first and most obvious way in which basic income makes us healthier. This pathway will be the topic of Chapter 2.

Second, basic income, by design, makes our livelihoods more predictable, certain and secure. This is, in fact, the main pragmatic reason for preferring it to other reforms that would have the same effect on the distribution of incomes. Predictability and certainty of material resources are, we contend, nearly as important as the level at which those resources are set. In particular, stress is intimately linked to uncertainty and unpredictability. The specific problems of early 21st-century capitalism – frequent changes of employment, the gig economy, multiple jobs, zero-hours contracts – entail what is often referred to as *precarity*.[26] This is just as much about uncertainty and unpredictability as it is about average wage levels. Chapter 3 sets out the case that uncertainty and unpredictability are leading causes of contemporary ill health, and that basic income is an excellent antidote.

Third, people facing extreme material need and irreducible uncertainty make certain kinds of decisions. They sometimes take bad risks. They are more likely than other people to use analgesic substances like tobacco, alcohol and other drugs. This is not to blame them for their predicament: their causes of their predicament are primarily structural. It is to understand that context affects decision making. Rational people don't weed their flower beds in war zones. Likewise, worrying about health effects of smoking that will become manifest decades later is the preserve of those who can at least be sure of getting through to the end of the month. If we make people's lives safer and more secure through basic income, a whole suite of behavioural changes will follow. These changes will have further beneficial consequences for population health and for the wellbeing of society. This is what behavioural scientist Gillian Pepper calls the *double dividend* of safety.[27] Structural reform improves population health directly, and then the members of the population, now having a better future they can rationally expect, start to change their behaviours in ways that yield even more health benefit, and hence save even more on the healthcare bill. The double dividend, and behavioural change more generally, is the topic of Chapter 4.

Whether you accept our case for basic income depends in part on whether you think the various beneficial effects traced in Figure 1.1 would really materialise. Each of those effects can be debated, but we did not just dream them up. There is a reasoned case that each of them would happen. Each case is supported by evidence from academic research.[28] Basic income has not yet been implemented anywhere in the world. The research therefore has to infer the likely consequences from a patchwork of sources: epidemiological studies of income and of health;[29] natural experiments like welfare system reforms and economic windfalls;[30] economic microsimulations;[31] and a small but growing set of experimental trials of schemes somewhat like basic income in populations smaller than a whole country.[32]

Our thinking about basic income goes beyond just asking whether the effects in Figure 1.1 would occur. We have also thought in detail about how big they would be: would they be large enough to make the scheme sustainable? For example, how much would be the saving to the NHS from better individual health?[33] How much might tax receipts go up due to reduced sickness and greater productivity?[34] The magnitudes, not just the directions, of all the knock-on changes matter a lot. We have considered these magnitudes in detail in our academic papers, and we will present some discussion of them later.

## Why is basic income superior to the alternatives?

You might be persuaded that some reform is needed to reduce poverty and improve population health. But why is basic income a better reform than the alternatives? The government has two major alternatives to ploughing money into basic income. It could improve the existing conditional welfare system, or it could devote more money to providing free or subsidised public services.

Conditional welfare systems require people to demonstrate that they meet some condition in order to receive a cash transfer. This applies to existing systems, like Universal Credit in the UK, and also to some hypothetical alternative systems that have been discussed, such as negative income tax and minimum income guarantee. In all these cases, the need to demonstrate eligibility poses problems. Applying is hard and stigmatising for claimants. For this reason, many people who are entitled to conditional benefits do not apply for them. It is also hard for the government: administrators need to make a huge number of judgement calls, often difficult around the boundaries, on eligibility. This requires a small army of assessors. In fact, it requires an army of assessors bigger than the actual army. At present, 81,600 people work for the Department for Work and Pensions.[35] The British army's regular strength is around 76,000.[36]

Assessing claims is a retrospective activity. As claimants, we have to show that, in the period leading up to the claim, we met the need condition. By the time the claim is assessed, this may no longer be the case. Any aid will come after the need was felt. What are we supposed to do in the meantime? In the gap, we may have had to take out high-interest loans, sell things we need, draw on the goodwill of friends who themselves may be facing hardship, or we just suffer and wait. We may have lost housing and been forced to travel to seek work. We may have had to go without food or to choose food over heating our homes. These things are obviously bad for our health and wellbeing, above and beyond the negative effects of being in need in the first place.

More than this, the outcome of the assessment of a claim for a conditional benefit is fundamentally uncertain. This is necessarily so, or the system would not be conditional in any meaningful sense. This uncertainty is pernicious. Uncertainty means stress, and stress is bad for health (see Chapter 3). Uncertainty also means people cannot make prudent or beneficial decisions. Not knowing whether the safety net will materialise or not disincentivises people from, for example, starting businesses that might be very successful, but could fail. It disincentivises those of us who currently receive benefits from taking on work whose duration or quality is not yet clear, since we cannot be sure that, if we leave the benefits system, we will be able to get back in in future if necessary.

Conditional systems based on means testing generate perverse incentives. If there is an income-based condition, then there will be a point on the income scale where most of any extra pound earned will be lost, because the loss of benefits that comes from being a bit better off eats up most of the extra earnings. The amount of the next pound earned that the government takes away is known as the marginal deduction rate. For a lone parent on UK minimum wage currently working 24 hours a week and receiving Universal Credit, the marginal deduction rate is 70 per cent, because of the way Universal Credit is tapered out as earnings increase.[37] This is a higher marginal deduction rate than that of someone on ten times the income. Yet we constantly hear how tax rates on high earnings are too high, and that this discourages endeavour. If the people who say this were intellectually consistent, they would want Universal Credit *not* to be taken away as earnings rise. In other words, they should want Universal Credit to be basic income.

High marginal deduction rates are not the only perverse incentives.[38] Where there are conditions based on sickness, people have material incentives to remain sick and inactive.[39] Given that conditional benefits are assessed on household rather than individual resources, they can generate incentives to break families up, in order for individuals to receive more overall. This is distorting and intrusive. The state should be neutral with regard to who, if anyone, we choose to live with.

Given all these obvious drawbacks, you might wonder why conditional systems are so widespread, and form the backbone of current UK institutions. There are two parts to our answer. Conditionality is to some extent intuitive: it seems right that people should get something only if they have either earned it or find themselves in need through no fault of their own. We will return to these intuitive moral justifications at the end of the chapter. The second part is that conditional systems made more sense in earlier phases of capitalism. For example, when the basic architecture of the current UK benefits system was designed, households mostly had a single breadwinner who stayed in the same job for a long time. When the breadwinner had a full-time job, the salary was generally sufficient to meet their family's basic needs. It therefore made some sense to compensate households only for the bad luck of cyclical unemployment, or work-preventing ill health. These were rare, easy to detect events.

The benefits system did not need to intervene in most lives, though the tax code did exempt the first portion of household income, the portion most clearly devoted to meeting basic material needs, from income tax.

Today, households are much more variable, employment is much more unstable, and inequality is higher. We change jobs often, or work in the gig economy, or cycle between multiple sources of income that are insufficient for our families to meet their basic needs. The epistemic problem (the problem of knowledge) that the government is trying to solve is a much more difficult one nowadays. Not, 'Has a rare unfortunate event occurred?'; but rather, 'Does the architecture of employment and life events enable the person to meet their basic needs, and do they deserve support if not?'. Under basic income, the epistemic problem would not be completely eliminated (the government still has to work out who is a legally entitled resident, as they currently do for the vote), but it becomes a very much simpler one.

The bad outcome that the system needs to mitigate is a different one too. Not, 'Has this person been prevented from working due to no fault of their own?'; but rather, 'Can this person keep their head above water, whether working or not?'. According to the Joseph Rowntree Foundation, 61 per cent of UK adults experiencing poverty now live in households where at least one person is in paid employment.[40] In 2023, 38 per cent of people who received Universal Credit had a job, and more lived in households where someone else did.[41] As we have already mentioned, a big part of the experience of disadvantage today is about uncertainty and insecurity as much as the average level of resources. Conditional systems have thus become particularly badly suited to the problems we face.

We now turn to the question of why the government should spend money on basic income as opposed to the provision of free or inexpensive public services. In fact, we think the government should do both. We are not arguing for a libertarian position, in which the state provides individuals with basic income and otherwise shrinks away, leaving everything else to the private-sector marketplace. This kind of argument for basic income has certainly been made, and libertarians are among the various political groupings who have been attracted to the policy.[42]

We, by contrast, envisage the government as continuing to be involved in the direct provision of healthcare, education, utilities and many other things.

What then is the right balance between government provision of basic income, and government provision of services? We see the two as complementary, each justifiable in different ways. Provision of services is good for ensuring the satisfaction of widely shared needs where there are increasing returns to scale, or network or monopoly properties. Examples include hospital networks, clean water and sewerage, energy, and schools. On the other hand, basic income recognises that people's needs are idiosyncratic and that autonomy is important. The state cannot know in detail, and should not take it upon itself to decide, what the most pressing need of person X or person Y is to make their life healthier right now. Person X and person Y are best placed to answer that. While some needs can be assumed to be collective (we all want to be able to be warm and to drink clean water), beyond that, people have very different notions of what it is to thrive. The government should facilitate the efficient satisfaction of the widely shared needs, but beyond this it should allow people considerable autonomy. Basic income facilitates autonomy. How you spend it is not policed. It is also, importantly, paid to individuals rather than households, meaning that individuals are neither penalised nor rewarded for their choices about relationships with others, and should in many cases be less beholden to other family members for their subsistence. Basic income thus ushers in a real and important form of freedom. We believe that freedom is an important component of living healthily.

### But is basic income morally right?

You may have read these pragmatic arguments and even been persuaded by them, but still have a nagging worry. It just does not seem *right* that people should get money for nothing, especially people who are not facing some kind of crisis. It seems more intuitive to make transfers only to people who have either done something to earn it, or at least demonstrated that they really need it.

We can loosen these intuitions in several ways. First, remember that basic income is only one arm of the system of transfers of resources between the government and the citizen. One of the things people will do to 'deserve' their basic income is to agree to pay income tax on whatever they earn. Currently (2024), most people pay no income tax on the first £12,570 of earnings. If you take the higher (40 per cent) rate of tax to be the 'full' rate, they don't start paying this until they earn £50,271 per year. People have not done anything to 'deserve' these allowances. We just collectively agree that it makes sense to allow people to meet their basic needs first before asking them to contribute more. Under our basic income schemes, the personal allowance would be removed, so you can think of basic income as simply replacing this implicit transfer with an explicit one. Why is basic income (giving people the money, then taking it away through income tax if they earn) superior to personal allowance (forgoing the right to tax them on the first part of their income)? Because basic income, unlike income tax allowance, is still there if your income suddenly drops to zero. It gives you a floor you are sure you can stand on when things change.

When basic income-like schemes have been trialled, people have not withdrawn from the labour market.[43] Basic income is basic; people's aspirations are high. Total inactivity is difficult to maintain. Most lottery winners continue to do paid work.[44] Basic income allows people to work more productively, because it gives them the headroom and security to, for example, retrain for something they would thrive in and be suited to, to mount a start-up, or move away from abusive or toxic work situations that make them sick. Knowing that people have basic income would force employers to make work conditions better. Under those improved conditions, most people would end up contributing more, not less, to the market economy.[45]

Basic income also gives people the flexibility to devote time to socially important activities that are not remunerated, like caring for family members, for which the state would otherwise be picking up the bill. It is bizarre that parenting is so wholly dismissed as a valuable social activity, simply because it is not paid within the market economy. Ensuring that the next generation is raised competently is of obvious intrinsic as well as instrumental value. But, for parenting activity to figure as important under the current way of valuing things, workers have to parent other people's kids and be paid for it, rather than just looking after their own.

The incoherence of rejecting basic income on the basis of 'reciprocity' – people must contribute something in order to receive something – is made clear when we consider that caring is not currently considered a contribution, whereas many socially harmful activities that happen to be recompensed through the market are considered as such. Corporate accountants pay tax on the income they declare, so meet the criterion of 'reciprocity'. However, they cost the Exchequer and society in general, through the tax avoidance that they facilitate, much more than they ever contribute. It is less reciprocity than parasitism.[46] When contribution is understood in a broader way, there is no reasonable concern that people will not 'contribute to society', or 'do anything useful' under basic income, any more than is true now.

Another point to make is that 'you are entitled to X if and only if you do Y' is only one of several different models that we have for distributing resources.[47] It does not apply to every kind of resource. The vote goes to all adults who register. The streets we walk on and the air we breathe are available without eligibility requirement. This makes intuitive sense. It is not just that it would be prohibitively complex to enforce some kind of conditionality. Streets and air seem obviously part of the shared, collective legacy of society, whose use *should* be available to anyone who is legitimately here. If air quality improves, we should all breathe the benefits.[48]

Our support for basic income is built mainly on its consequences. These are so desirable and so broad as to make the policy make sense. Other writers have built cases on more abstract moral rules.[49] One example goes as follows. The fact that society today is starting from a high level of economic development is not deserved by the people who are economically active today. Fertile farmland, good roads, good educational institutions, an electricity grid, a (mostly) functional sewerage network, and a high level of literacy and sophistication in the population were not *earned* by anyone alive today. These good things arose gradually through the luck of a temperate climate, and the collective efforts of an indefinitely large set of people all doing their thing over hundreds of years. They provided us, unwittingly, with a *legacy*. We – regardless of our generation – came into the world and essentially got this legacy as a windfall. The legacy produces an enormous and ongoing flow of riches, a flow that would not happen without it.

Now, who owns the legacy of society? Who deserves it? Surely the doctor or the banker don't own it any more than the unemployed single parent does. But the doctor and the banker do *benefit* from it more. The doctor and the banker, through the vicissitudes of individual characteristics and opportunity, can convert that legacy into private wealth and social power, more so than some others can. Yes, effort is involved in this process, but those efforts would come to nought without the legacy, which they got for free but helps them disproportionately, as well as protecting their gains from it once they have made them.

We think it is ethically right that everyone should be given the fair value of their share in the social legacy. After that, social processes can take their course. In short, just being a member of society gives you a partial claim on the bounty of society. In this way, basic income is not just morally justifiable in its provision; it is morally questionable in its being withheld. For this reason, we feel that well-meaning proposals like the 'participation income', which is like basic income but requires recipients to 'do something for society', like working, caring or volunteering, are misguided. They fail practically, because of the mind-boggling difficulties of monitoring and enforcement, and morally, in that people have a real *un*conditional moral claim on part of the common wealth.

What about the moral *consequences* for society of introducing basic income? Some people fear that it would be morally corrosive. For example, it might undermine individual responsibility, or tempt people to indulge in drink or drugs. We think the opposite is true. Where cash transfer schemes that resemble basic income have been studied, the use of temptation goods such as narcotics goes *down* rather than up, as do antisocial behaviours in general.[50] When you give people lives they can control, and reasonable hopes for the future, they need anxiety- and pain-numbing chemicals less, not more, and they have less reason to destroy the things around them. There are downsides to making large, rare payments, such as once a year, as happens with the Alaska Permanent Fund Dividend, a yearly payment derived from investment of the state's oil revenue.[51] Payment season can see an uptick in accidental deaths and overdoses. We see this as an argument for providing basic income as a smaller but more frequent and predictable weekly payment.

More generally, people can only be morally responsible where they operate freely. We would not usually criticise someone for acts they committed with a gun to their head, because we know their actions are not free. Economic desperation – for example, severe hunger or the fear of imminent eviction – undermines freedom in this sense. This is what Thomas Jefferson described as the 'moral coercion of want'.[52] Inadequacy of resources makes people slaves to their situations, and to the arbitrary whims of others. Desperate circumstances make people do all kinds of things that run against their reasoned preferences. The judicial system contains a mixture of people who made morally repugnant decisions, and people who faced desperate circumstances. If we eliminated the non-freedom that comes from desperate want, we would live in a more moral society: one in which everyone could be held accountable for their actions, because they were more likely to have chosen those actions freely.

What a morally good society looks like is a question much broader than the scope of this book. People want different things out of life, and society should allow for this plurality. A reasonable general principle is that in a good society, people are not subject to arbitrary domination by the will of others.[53] For this reason and others, we have laws against aggression, coercion, slavery and discrimination. However, fully realising freedom requires more than just laws to protect us from interference. It also requires insulation from the vulnerability that might make us have to do things we otherwise would not want to do. Basic income is an important form of insulation from domination of this kind. Moreover, removing domination by want does not just make us freer. It makes us healthier, too.

You might well disagree with the foregoing moral arguments for basic income. You might still be thinking, 'Well, it's tough luck,

## Why basic income?

but if people don't work, and then have poor health or do bad things, that's their fault and they need to bear the consequences.' Though we do not agree, we understand the intuition: it coherently applies one way of thinking about responsibility and obligation. If we have not been able to convince you to think differently about the morality of the case, we would still fall back on our pragmatic arguments. We ask you to consider whether you would still hold your rigid moral position even in the knowledge that upholding it means the society you live in will be more unhealthy, more violent and more unhappy than it need be. We ask you: are you prepared to bear the consequences of your belief?[54] The costs are extraordinarily great in public health, crime, education and civil decline.

In our view, it is not poor people, but poverty and the threat of poverty, which are immoral. As Milton Friedman, hardly a bleeding-heart leftie, put it: '[T]he people whose freedom is really being interfered with [under the status quo] are the poor ... they are the people who are deprived of personal liberty, freedom, and dignity.'[55] That other darling of those who are anti-government, Friedrich Hayek, also favoured putting a floor under people's incomes. He saw a fundamental moral benefit of doing so, running alongside the pragmatic ones:

> The assurance of a certain minimum income for everyone, or a sort of floor below which nobody need fall even when he is unable to provide for himself, appears not only to be a wholly legitimate protection against a risk common to all, but a necessary part of the Great Society.[56]

**Case Study: Young people's views of the moral implications of basic income in Bradford**

In Bradford, young people described the daily emotional and moral tolls that poverty and inequality take on their lives. One man from the 21–24-year-old age group claimed that their 'main emotion is just stress and anxiety': '[It] sort of makes you feel like crap, especially when everyone around you has so much money in comparison to you ...

[It's] really embarrassing to explain to people that you can't do things. ... And then they look down at you.'

A woman from the 21–24 age group reported her family's experience of the benefits system: '[W]e didn't want to admit that we needed the help and support and we didn't want to live on benefits. And then the whole process of applying for it was really complicated and confusing as well. ... We were very depressed for a long time.'

A girl from the 14–16 age group noted that 'Sometimes when I ask for money from my parents, I kind of feel guilty anyway, because I'm taking away money that they need for essentials and to help us have a roof over our heads.'

These are moral quandaries that young people are being confronted with for the first time in generations, in a country that is increasingly poor with a few extremely rich residents.[57] This generation of young people has a position on wealth and basic income that reflects the much more difficult circumstances that they have experienced than their parents and even grandparents. Whereas older people are more likely to refer to moral issues regarding taxing wealthier Britons, participants in the workshops noted that 'Inequality is rising in the UK and reducing the gap should be a priority for society' and were centrally concerned with the moral question of whether 'rich friends', 'people with generational wealth' or 'the middle class' should receive payments that they do not need. One female 16–18-year-old participant felt that the 'upper class' already have enough money and that basic income would therefore not be directed to people that truly need it. Such concerns were alleviated when it was explained that basic income is paired with progressive taxation. As one man from the 21–24 group concluded, 'All of us would be more happy, not just one of us. All a tiny bit happier everyday. ... There is [an] amplifier effect if everyone is happy.' A woman from the same group added that people having more money 'would have a knock-on effect for their health [and] the NHS wouldn't be as strained as it is ... I feel like there's a lot of like ripple effects that would happen'. These sorts of pragmatic arguments played the central role in determining young people's moral support for basic income.

*2*

# Securing the basics: reducing poverty

This chapter focuses on the first set of desirable effects of basic income, the effects that come about because basic income reduces poverty. Poverty is the situation where material resources are insufficient in amount to fulfil basic needs. For the UK, the poverty line is often set at the household income corresponding to 60 per cent of the national median. To reduce poverty, therefore, you need to boost the incomes of those households who are around or below this line (around a fifth of households). We will show that all of our schemes, even scheme 1, give a very substantial income boost to households in poverty in particular.

You might be confused at this point: if everyone receives the same basic income payment, then surely everyone's income goes up by the same amount? This is not really the case: the effects are very different depending on our personal situations. For one thing, we live in households of different sizes. Basic income is paid to each adult, and for each child, so a household of two adults and three children will receive more from it than a household of one or two adults and no children. Larger households are more likely to be in poverty. Also, the introduction of basic income will be accompanied by changes to income tax. For some people the tax increases will be smaller than the basic income gain, and for others it will be the other way around (the highest-income households will be net payers-in, despite receiving their weekly payments). As we will show, the worse off you are at present, the greater the uplift in your income will be when the combined effects of the basic income and the tax changes are added together. And, because those of us with the lowest incomes are starting from a lower baseline, the *proportional* gain will of course be greatest at the bottom end of the income distribution.

All this means, counterintuitively perhaps, that although basic income makes the same payment to everyone, its net effects on incomes end up very precisely targeted at lifting low-income households out of poverty. This chapter will also address the question of why reducing poverty is such an important goal. We will argue that reducing poverty – the ultimate 'levelling up' – is justified not solely by appeal to moral principle or altruism, but also because it will partly pay for itself. By stimulating economic activity, it will increase tax revenues; by making us healthier, it will produce significant savings on healthcare and social costs.

To predict the effects of basic income on poverty, the numbers matter. We need to model how it would benefit households of every possible combination of composition and income, as well as knowing how prevalent each of these household types is. This means building a detailed simulation, based on the best available data, of what UK households are currently like, and what their incomes and tax liabilities would look like after the scheme is introduced. We have been working on this question for several years, and in this chapter we draw on a series of our academic publications.[1] We warn you, however, that the numbers stem from 2023 and in some cases 2022. In the interim (we are writing in 2024), there has been considerable inflation and a certain amount of economic change. We also draw on a couple of different publications that were themselves prepared some months apart. The numbers should therefore be taken as indicative.

## Basic income payments go to everyone, but their net effects are targeted

We have simulated the impacts of our basic income schemes, with their accompanying income tax changes, on household incomes for households in each decile of the income distribution. A decile is a tenth part of the overall distribution of households. Thus, decile one contains the household with the very lowest income through to the household for whom 90 per cent of households have higher income than them and 10 per cent lower; and the tenth decile that contains the household for whom 90 per cent of households have lower income than them, through to the household with the very highest income. If you are curious roughly which decile your household might belong to, you can check online calculators such as that hosted by the IFS.[2] The simulations take into account the different compositions of households at different deciles of the income distribution.

Table 2.1 summarises the results of our simulations by showing the percentage change in income, compared to the status quo, for every decile of UK household incomes, under each scheme. Let us take scheme 1 for illustration. At the lower extreme of the income distribution (decile 1, and into decile 2) lie households with minimal or very low earned income. Their incomes will be strongly boosted by the introduction of scheme 1. A household containing two working-age adults and two children would receive a total of £250 a week. This means a chunk of households would get more than they do under the current Universal Credit and Child Benefit regimes. Many of them are currently failing to consistently get payments out of Universal Credit anyway, because they are fined for condition violations, because their situations often change, or because of the difficulty and stigma of claiming. This group of households – those who are in or close to poverty – are the big gainers from scheme 1.

Above this extreme lie layers of households who are currently managing, to varying degrees. They have a decent amount of earned income. Depending on the size of this, they may be getting some help from Universal Credit as well, and many are getting Child Benefit. Scheme 1 increases their liabilities to the government a little, through the loss of personal allowances and slightly higher tax rates. But this is offset by the basic income cash coming in. They are also freed from high marginal deduction rates. Households in these layers – the majority of UK households – go from benefiting moderately, in the lower strata like decile 3, to being unaffected on balance, in the higher ones, like decile 8.

At the top of the income distribution lie households containing people with large incomes from salaries, bonuses or capital gains. These households – especially the top decile – will experience a non-trivial net income loss from the introduction of scheme 1. This is because the increases in their tax liabilities will be larger than the for-them modest payment they will receive. It is

**Table 2.1:** Percentage changes in household income compared to the status quo, for each of the basic income schemes

| Decile of household incomes | Scheme 1 | Scheme 2 | Scheme 2 completely recouped through income tax | Scheme 3 | Scheme 3 completely recouped through income tax |
|---|---|---|---|---|---|
| 1 (lowest) | +139.5 | +324.2 | +319.5 | +533.6 | +519.9 |
| 2 | +8.2 | +22.7 | +19.2 | +50.1 | +39.6 |
| 3 | +3.8 | +15.1 | +10.4 | +36.3 | +21.7 |
| 4 | +4.1 | +14.7 | +9.2 | +34.1 | +17.1 |
| 5 | +3.2 | +11.5 | +5.6 | +29.5 | +11.4 |
| 6 | +3.6 | +12.2 | +5.8 | +31.7 | +11.9 |
| 7 | +2.5 | +11.6 | +4.3 | +31.4 | +8.7 |
| 8 | −0.1 | +10.6 | +2.0 | +30.0 | +3.4 |
| 9 | −2.4 | +6.5 | −3.4 | +23.0 | −7.1 |
| 10 (highest) | −7.0 | −5.2 | −16.8 | +5.0 | −30.5 |

Source: H.R. Reed, M.T. Johnson, S. Lansley, E.A. Johnson, G. Stark and K.E. Pickett, 'Universal Basic Income is Affordable and Feasible: Evidence from UK Economic Microsimulation Modelling', *The Journal of Poverty and Social Justice* 31, no. 1 (2023): 146–162.

important to be clear about this, since an objection we sometimes hear to basic income is that it seems to be giving money to rich people who do not need it. In fact, evaluating the distributional effect overall, this is not the case. Scheme 1 takes from the highest-income households to give to the rest, and especially to those with the lowest incomes. It is thus a redistributive measure, despite the payments coming at the same flat rate for everyone.

Schemes 2 and 3 have broadly the same profile of impacts as scheme 1, with a group of very low-income households gaining a huge amount, a middle group gaining modestly, and a top group who are net payers-in. We have simulated schemes 2 and 3 under two different assumptions. Under the first, we assume they would be paid for through expenditure savings or revenue streams other than personal income taxation. Under the second, we assume that personal income tax rates would have to be set such as to recoup all the cost of the scheme (this is also the assumption we used for scheme 1). We make the personal income tax rates progressive in either case.

# Securing the basics: reducing poverty

To summarise the table, this policy is dramatically transformational for the households with the lowest incomes. It is somewhat good for the incomes of all the people in the middle. And it will cost something for the households at the top. These figures are important because what most people seem to want out of the benefits system is that it helps the worst off the most. People's preferences are what are described in the jargon as 'quasi-maximin' or 'quasi-Rawlsian'.[3] This means that people are particularly attentive to the effect of a policy on the least well-off: they want to make the benefit to that group as big as possible. Basic income does this, as Table 2.1 shows.

Scheme 1 would reduce the incidence of child poverty from the current 27.3 per cent of children to 12.5 per cent, and working-age poverty from 19.4 per cent to 14.9 per cent. These are huge changes by any historical standard. Scheme 3 would create much more substantial change than that, seeing child poverty dwindle to 3.8 per cent of children and working-age poverty to 5.9 per cent. These percentages are only as high as they are because the conventional definition of the poverty line is set at 60 per cent of the median household income. This median would be much higher under scheme 3, so we would see a smaller proportion of people fall below a much higher bar.

Most people believe that current levels of inequality in the UK are too high. Inequality would be substantially reduced under any of the schemes. The Gini coefficient measures the degree of inequality of the income distribution, with zero representing the case of perfect equality, and one representing the case where one household has all of the income. Under our calculations, the UK's Gini coefficient would fall from 0.35 to 0.30 even under scheme 1.[4] A Gini difference of 0.05 is greater than the current difference between the UK and Denmark, by one calculation.[5]

## Why is reducing poverty such an important priority?

The previous section established that a basic income scheme would efficiently reduce poverty and inequality. This raises the question: why is this the right goal for the government to have? There are many worthwhile claims on the government's action, including mitigating climate change, improving municipal services and fixing the education system. We believe, however, that there is a special priority to be accorded to poverty reduction (and the related reduction in inequality) in the period through which we are living.

One reason is that the prevalence of poverty has, overall, been going in the wrong direction for decades. In 1961 an estimated 9 per cent of working-age parents and 6 per cent of working-age non-parents were below the poverty line. By 2022–2023, these figures were 17 per cent and 13 per cent.[6] Relatedly, the Gini coefficient has increased by 0.10 over the same period (so, our scheme 1 only undoes about half of the impact of the last 60 years). Scholarship and media discussion on poverty tends to focus on the character and behaviour of individual people, but the main determinant of the rate of poverty in countries like the UK is government policy. In places and times where governments devote resources to generous, broad-based social safety nets, the rate of poverty is correspondingly lowered.[7] Poverty has increased in the UK because of the public policies that have been enacted; our schemes go some way to reversing this.

The rising rate of poverty matters not just because poverty offends our sensibilities. It also matters because poverty makes people sick. When you measure income and health in the same population, there is always a correlation. Those with lower incomes have shorter lives, worse self-reported health, more conditions that need treatment, more need of the National Health Service, and greater physical and psychological pain. This correlation survives statistical correction for pretty much all the things we can think of. The shape of the relationship between income and health is non-linear, with a steeper increase in health per extra pound earned for those on the lowest incomes.[8] This bodes well for our basic income schemes, which, as we have shown, benefit this group the most.

However, it is one thing to observe a reliable correlation. It is another thing to know what it means in causal terms. It could be that poverty makes you sick. It could also be having health problems, for whatever reason, causes your income to decline over time. For a long time, people could shy away from what seems like the obvious conclusion – that inadequate income is a fundamental cause of ill health – by saying that correlation is not causation, and that the causality might be the other way around. Causal interpretation matters for intervention. If you doubt that there is a causal arrow from income to health, you will not believe that boosting the incomes of poor people will increase the health of the population.

By now, however, it is becoming hard not to conclude that lower income causes worse health. The reverse pathway is real too: people who suffer long-term health problems do often see their careers and incomes stall or reverse. But there are several lines of evidence that increasing incomes lead to changes in health states. We will discuss these very briefly in what follows. You will note we do not make much distinction between physical and mental health (some of the evidence uses physical health outcomes, others more mental). This is not us playing fast and loose. Rather, physical and mental health difficulties tend to cluster together in the same individuals.[9] People with depression and other common mental disorders die younger.[10] It is the same syndrome of life-threatening ill health.

The first source of evidence is from longitudinal studies. Here, researchers look at the same individuals over time to discover how *changes* in their incomes are associated with *changes* in health, generally finding that health improves in the wake of income increasing.[11] This is still not conclusive proof of causality, but it is suggestive. In a recent study in the UK and France, we tracked people's financial situations and their mental health every month for a year.[12] The participants' symptoms of depression and anxiety fluctuated in lockstep with the money going into their bank accounts: fewer symptoms at the end of a month where they had had a bit more coming in than usual, and more symptoms in months that had been lean. The straightforward interpretation of this finding is that their financial situations were directly driving their mental health states, without much of a time lag at all. We have reached similar conclusions in a much larger UK population study (over years, not months) using both mental and physical health outcomes.[13]

The second source of evidence exploits changes in public policies that affect the poverty rate. These studies are sometimes described as 'natural experiments', because the changes in policy are external to the people affected, and they happen abruptly, at well-defined places and times. For example, studies have looked at temporal changes in welfare regimes in several countries, including the UK, New Zealand and the United States.[14] The regimes become more or less generous in real terms as governments change. Increased generosity reduces the poverty rate, and reduces the excess mortality and ill health of people on lower incomes. Decreased generosity does the opposite.

Epidemiologist Clare Bambra looked for historical cases where the health and life expectancy gap between people in the lowest and highest socioeconomic positions in a society narrowed rapidly.[15] She found five: the Nordic countries from the 1950s to the 1970s; the United States in the 1960s; Brazil in the 1980s; Germany after reunification in the 1990s; and, to a more modest degree, the UK in the 2000s under the government of Tony Blair. Bambra identifies three features common to all five cases. Two of the features were better access to healthcare, and greater political inclusion for the most disadvantaged groups (the working class in social democratic postwar Scandinavia, African Americans in the civil rights era). The other one, importantly for our purposes, was that in *all* the cases, the incomes of the most disadvantaged people were raised, often in non-conditional ways. The Nordic countries enacted universal and comparatively generous benefits; the United States in the 1960s saw Lyndon Johnson's 'war on poverty'; Brazil in the 1980s saw the introduction of the '*bolsa família*' (a cash transfer to poor families); Germany, upon reunification, gave Western-level pensions to Eastern retirees, and it was among retirees that the rapid health gain occurred; the Blair government introduced the national minimum wage and more support for families. Bambra describes the relationship between welfare provision and health improvement as dose-response: the better people are protected from poverty, the closer the health of the least well-off is to the health of the best-off. Where the policies were unpicked or reversed, health inequalities become worse again. Bambra's work reinforces the comments made here, that in affluent democracies, government policies constitute the main cause of poverty, and the most effective antidote; and shows that the effects of policies bleed through to health outcomes.

The third source of evidence is cash transfer trials. These have acquired something of a special status in the basic income

## Securing the basics: reducing poverty

community because they are (more or less) true experiments – some people are assigned to get payments, and there is usually a control group that does not – and the transfer schemes look at least somewhat like basic incomes. However, we must not forget that these trials have a lot of limitations. The payments are typically for a limited period, and the participants know this. The experiments introduce payments, but not the changes to the taxation system that would go alongside them in a true basic income. And, the experiments do not usually happen at the scale of a whole population. This means that we cannot assess any synergistic benefit (or drawback) that comes from a person experiencing not being poor, and none of the people around them being poor either. The cash transfer evidence comes predominantly, though not exclusively, from lower- and middle-income countries, and none comes from the UK.

Nonetheless, the picture across a sizeable set of trials is that increasing income experimentally via cash transfers improves health, probably quite substantially so. In one Canadian trial, which took place at the scale of a whole town, the probability of hospitalisation reduced by 8.5 per cent,[16] which is a large change (think of your local hospital being attended by 8.5 per cent fewer people on a given day). Averaging across the low- and middle-income country trials, the risk of having had any illness in the preceding few weeks is reduced by 20 per cent.[17] Anyone who works in population health will tell you that this is a huge effect: we are used to trying to squeeze out very marginal improvements. The effects of cash interventions on mental health states are the best documented and most consistent.[18]

## The payback from poverty reduction

If the preceding section has persuaded you that reducing poverty would improve health, then there is a payoff that will come to society and to the government when poverty is reduced. To try to quantify this payoff, we used data from the UK Household Longitudinal Study, also known as Understanding Society.[19] This is a nationally representative cohort of British people whose financial situations and health status has been followed for 12 years. We used a subset of about 7,000 of them to estimate the effects of income changes on physical and mental health. We did this by looking at how people's health changes when their income changes. We then plugged these estimated effects into our economic microsimulation of the whole UK population, and saw what would happen if our basic income schemes were introduced. Naturally, these estimates carry considerable uncertainty. Our methods model the immediate health effects of a financial change; they take no account of ways that effects of low income on health might cumulate, perhaps non-linearly, over time. Also, they take no account of any beneficial health effects of basic income other than the effects on the level of individual incomes, or any effects on the health of children.

Using these methods, we estimate that the introduction of scheme 1 would prevent or postpone around 124,000 cases of depression and 118,000 cases of physical health problems, per year. You can convert these numbers into Quality Adjusted Life Years (QALYs), which is used by health economists to compare the social and economic impact of different health interventions. One QALY is equivalent to one person having an extra year of life in perfect health. An extra year of life spent in poor health, or the conversion of a year in poor health to a year in moderate health, is worth some fraction of a QALY. When we do the sums, we obtain an estimate of around 129,000 QALYs per year gained from scheme 1. In cost–benefit analyses, QALYs are often given a nominal value of £30,000. This is supposed to represent the reduction in healthcare cost and the increase in productivity from health gains. Valuing QALYs allows for policies with health implications to be assessed in terms of cost-effectiveness. At this valuation, the health 'benefit' of scheme 1, via poverty reduction, is estimated at £3.87 billion per year. The payoffs for scheme 3 are dramatically higher, at 655,000 QALYS worth almost £20 billion per year.

The £3.87 billion figure is a substantial proportion of the cost of the scheme 1 payments. But remember, scheme 1 was *already* fiscally neutral through the changes to the tax code. The £3.87 billion represents, if you like, a windfall on a scheme that has already paid for itself. Here we see, and later chapters will elaborate, the way basic income is not just a cost: it is also a generator of collective return.

## Case Study: Impacts on Blyth

Research with our partners in Blyth's regeneration and public health programmes revealed a town of contrasts – great community spirit, civic pride and natural resources, together with disabling rates of chronic health problems and neighbourhoods counted among the 1 per cent most deprived in England.[20] Those living in the centre of Blyth talk about there being 'no way out' of the confines of Universal Credit, an empty town centre and the shocking realities of living hand to mouth in poorly maintained houses, owned by private landlords they have never met. In blunt terms, as reported by *The Times* newspaper, 'Nee bugga gives a shit about us.'[21]

While 'Levelling Up' monies are spent in Blyth principally on physical infrastructure projects, the day to day realities of living on a low income continue to hit hard, leaving local newspapers to describe fears of the creation of a 'ghost town'.[22] Eileen Cartie, manager of the Buffalo Community Centre, told us that 'choosing between heating and eating is a reality for many families we support. People don't just "get by" on very low incomes, they are left not knowing what's going to happen next'. The families Eileen supports desperately need the uplift – and greater certainty – that would result from eradicating low incomes. A basic income would turn the focus of the town away from foodbanks and charity shops, to positive stories of new entrepreneurs, a creative culture and an opportunity for those on lowest incomes to plan pathways to work in the town's burgeoning renewable industries.

3

# Freedom from stress

It is something of a commonplace that we live in an age of stress. In a 2021 survey, 79 per cent of adults in the UK said they felt stressed at least once a month; 49 per cent at least five days a month; and 30 per cent ten or more days a month.[1] The under-55s were notably more stressed than the over-55s. Finances and work loomed very large in the list of things people attributed the stress to. It is hard to benchmark these numbers. There are no long-term time series of how stressed people in the UK have felt. The concept of stress as we use it today was only coined in the 1930s and did not become widespread in everyday language until much more recently. In earlier times, people surely experienced distress and upset, even if they used a different vocabulary to understand and communicate it. Moreover, even in the healthiest imaginable society, there will be stress: people will always have first dates and professional goals and political frustrations that they get worked up over.

Nonetheless, many people agree that, despite material affluence, something about stress is out of kilter in the UK and other Western countries in the current time.[2] Stress is a not a psychiatric disorder, but it is a risk factor for common psychiatric disorders.[3] These disorders are more widely diagnosed and treated than in the past. Stress is also a risk factor for physical illness, perhaps especially for men.[4] Stress seems to play a role in maintaining the gradient whereby physical illness (and death) come earlier for those with lower incomes and worse jobs.[5] The contention of this chapter is that basic income is the right policy antidote for this excess of stress, a better antidote than the conceivable alternatives. This is not just because of the effects of basic income on poverty and inequality that we discussed in Chapter 2, but also because of an additional consequence of basic income: it reduces uncertainty about future resources. This uncertainty effect is logically distinct from the distributional effect (that is, basic income's tendency to increase the overall incomes of those at the bottom of the distribution). The uncertainty-reducing effect of basic income thus provides a separate pathway through which it will be good for health. This means, importantly, that basic income will have a healthy uncertainty-reducing effect even for people towards the top of the income distribution, whose incomes will be no higher after its introduction, because their basic income will be completely outweighed by tax changes. This chapter will explain why this is the case. First, though, we need to consider the concept of stress, and the reasons it arises.

## What is stress?

Stress is both a psychological and a physiological concept. There is some link between the two: the hormone cortisol is secreted into the blood when someone faces a challenge they find psychologically stressful. This leads to several metabolic and circulatory changes. However, cortisol is not well described as the 'stress' hormone. Its function is better described as 'mobilizing metabolic energy to allow the organism to do something'.[6] That something could include coping with a nasty psychological stressor, but could also include waking up and getting out of bed, going for a run or having sex. If we want to understand the kind of stress that people find unpleasant, and that has negative long-term health impacts – in short, the kind of stress that is out of balance in the contemporary UK – we need to identify what stress means at the psychological level. In doing so, we need to bear in mind that there is a health difference between acute stress, which is short term, and chronic stress, which is longer term and often less noticeable to us as we become accustomed to it.[7]

For a situation to be experienced as psychologically stressful, two conditions need to be met. First, the person needs to be under some *uncertainty* about what will end up happening. It is not stressful if the outcome is completely known in advance, even if the outcome is sad or regrettable. Second, some of the possible outcomes must be bad. By bad, we mean that they constitute a threat to the person's wellbeing. Thus, stress can be defined as uncertainty in a context in which there are potential threats.

This definition does a good job at capturing where and when people say they feel stressed. For example, in a recent experiment, participants had to repeatedly predict whether an image of a rock would be followed by an image of a snake or not.[8] If there was an image of a snake, they would receive an unpleasant electric shock to their left hand. Over the course of the long experiment, the probability of snakes varied: sometimes there were never snakes, sometimes there were always snakes, and sometimes it was unpredictable whether there would be a snake or not. Every few rocks, the participants were asked how stressed they felt right now.

People's stress ratings closely tracked their uncertainty about whether there would be a snake behind the next rock or not. They were less stressed by actually getting shocked than by not knowing whether they would get shocked or not. The most stressful phase of the experiment was not the one with the most shocks, but the one where the probability of there being a snake behind the rock was 50 per cent: then you really have no idea whether a shock is coming or not, so your uncertainty is maximal. This experiment was just the latest in a long line of findings highlighting the specific role of uncertainty in the experience of stress[9] and discomfort. Interestingly, the researchers found that people who believed the experimental world to be more volatile (the researchers could estimate this from their snake-prediction patterns) were also those who reported the most life stress outside the experiment. The researchers took this to mean that the people who had the most uncertainty in their real lives brought that uncertainty into the experimental context.

Once we understand the central role of uncertainty in the psychological stress response, the relationship between the psychological and physiological senses of stress becomes clearer. The reason that psychological stress triggers cortisol release is that dealing with uncertainty requires energy. At the very least, you need to fuel brain activity to try to figure out and mitigate whatever is going to happen.[10] You may need to fight, flee or take other kinds of remedial physical action. Whatever happens, uncertainty in the context of threat requires you to spend energy, energy that you could otherwise be husbanding or saving for other functions, including the functions involved in keeping healthy. This is why chronic stress is so damaging to health in the long term. The energy that threatening uncertainty requires of you must be taken out of the energy budget available for everything else. The term burnout in the context of chronic psychosocial stress may well be a literal one: you burned through the energy that you needed to use to keep yourself healthy.

Uncertainty generates stress, and stress is unpleasant. People avoid unpleasant things where they can. People are therefore, usually, averse to risk and averse to uncertainty.[11] Aversion to risk means that people prefer £100 for sure to flipping a coin where they would win £250 if it came up heads. Aversion to uncertainty means preferring a gamble whose odds are known to a gamble whose odds are unknown but could be better. However, individuals cannot entirely avoid risk and uncertainty all on their own. Good institutions ought to help.

The central role of uncertainty in psychological stress has important implications for social policy. It means that the health and wellbeing outcomes of a person who receives £1,000 a month and is certain that this will happen will be better than that of a person who in fact receives £1,000 a month, but is uncertain ahead of time that they will do so. Therefore, two social policies, X and Y, could have exactly the same effects on the distribution of incomes in the population, but still be different in terms of their effects on stress, health and wellbeing. The superior policy would be the one that generated less uncertainty.

### Resource streams, uncertainty and precarity

Your material resources are made up of both a stock and a flow. The stock might include your savings and assets like your house. The flow is the income you receive each month, whether from wages, self-employment, pensions or benefits. For most people in the UK, the stock is not nearly big enough to live on for the rest of their lives. They depend on the flow continuing to flow.

The flow of material resources has two parts, a certain part and an uncertain part. For example, several of the authors of this book are university professors. For them, the certain part is large, and the uncertain part is small. The certain part, for them, consists of decent salaries that don't change much from year to year, from jobs that go on (and on). The uncertain part consists of perhaps a few hundred pounds from a guest lecture from time to time. This is an unimportant proportion of the total, but it is nonetheless uncertain: the amount is different from month to month, and it is hard to predict in advance in which months it might be higher.

For people with other kinds of jobs (often low-paying ones, to boot), the uncertain part of their income stream is much more important relative to the certain part. Zero-hours contracts, for example, evoke uncertainty about how much one will earn from week to week. Self-employment does the same from month to month. So too do short-term jobs and jobs paid piece by piece – the so-called 'gig economy'. Zero-hours contracts and self-employment have increased in the UK in recent years.[12]

The relative sizes of the certain and uncertain parts of the income stream matter. Where the certain part is enough to meet one's basic needs and obligations every month, one is insulated from serious economic threat: any uncertainty is relatively unimportant. Where the uncertain part is the bulk of one's income, this is not so. The problem British people have is not just that many of them are too poor, though this is true for some. Many more of them are *uncertain* that they can make ends meet from one month to the next. They probably will, in most cases in most months, but they are at least somewhat uncertain about it. Thus, many British people find themselves in what Guy Standing felicitously dubbed 'the precariat'.[13]

Being in the precariat is stressful, and hence bad for health. The evidence for this comes from a growing number of studies showing that volatility in income streams leads to bad health, even after adjusting for the overall amount of money in the stream.[14] A highly volatile stream is one that changes a lot over time. Presumably the health effects are due to the volatility generating uncertainty, which generates stress. We suggest that the reason that 'stress' is such a defining term for our current age is that people are responding psychologically to the increased volatility and uncertainty of the labour market compared to 50 or even 20 years ago.

## The current welfare system exacerbates uncertainty

You would hope that our main safety net, the welfare state, would reduce uncertainty. That should be one of its functions. To some extent, it does seem to work; a larger welfare state seems to reduce uncertainty compared to a smaller one. In a recent analysis, Macchia and Oswald looked at levels of worry expressed in large polls by residents of Organisation for Economic Co-operation and Development (OECD) countries in the last couple of decades. They find that an important predictor of worry is the level of government social spending – broadly, spending on the welfare state.[15] When this spending goes down, worry goes up, and when this spending goes up, worry goes down. Part of the reason for the overall increase in worry in recent years in multiple countries seems to be welfare state retrenchment.

The fact that the welfare state is somewhat effective in reducing worry (and presumably uncertainty) does not mean that its current design is the best available one. The UK welfare system has, as it stands, several features that increase rather than decrease uncertainty. It increases uncertainty because the person who finds themselves unable to meet their basic needs must apply, retrospectively, for support. There is then a delay, of variable duration, while the application is assessed. Now there is uncertainty both in the amount of resource (will my application be approved, or not?) and in delay (when will the resource show up?). Even if the application is approved, it may be reassessed periodically, sometimes as much as every month. Our experience with the benefits system is that people are very unclear when such a reassessment process might happen or what is responsible for triggering it, let alone determining the result.

The conditionality of the system introduces further uncertainty. Where there are behavourial conditions like the need to seek work, the person may have the benefit withdrawn at any time if they are deemed not to have complied well enough (these penalties are known as sanctions). To take another example, imagine that a person on Universal Credit decides to take a job which is somewhat casual, a classic gig economy gig. The amount of work and earnings that this will generate in practice is uncertain. But so is the response of the benefits system. Will the benefits system correctly compensate for the ups and downs in the new income stream? When exactly will Universal Credit be withdrawn? And, if the paid work dries up, how quickly and easily will the person be able to get back onto Universal Credit? In effect, for the person who has managed to get onto Universal Credit and is averse to uncertainty, it is more appealing *not* to take the work, because of all the uncertainty generated by the possible withdrawal and reinstatement of the benefit. Thus, the conditional system is not ideal from the point of view of stress (which is what we are primarily concerned about) *or* from the point of view of incentives to take paid work (which the government and media often say they care about).

There is also something particularly psychologically ugly and demeaning about the conditional benefits system, which is the following. Exposure to uncontrollable uncertainty is unpleasant, but exposure to uncontrollable uncertainty generated by the whim of another person is particularly awful. This is why the experience of powerlessness is so terrible, and why unaccountable hierarchy is so psychologically destructive. One of our group members in Jarrow described the indignity and stress of being assessed and re-assessed very vividly:

> To me, a basic income would feel far more dignified. I mean, we've been through some awful things. Still going through them … I get people every four years coming to my house asking whether I'm still as blind as I was four years previously … and a lot of our income … hinges on that. So that happens every four years, which is stressful … because straightaway … you know they're coming from a point of view of 'we don't trust you'.

Freedom, in its most useful sense, involves not being beholden to the arbitrary whim of someone else. The opposite of freedom is domination. Domination is psychologically damaging. It has been present, of course, throughout human history, to greater or lesser degrees in different times and places. But a good use we could make of our unprecedented material affluence might be to progressively reduce domination to the minimum feasible level.

In any conditional benefits system, claimants are subject to the will of a decision maker, as memorably dramatised in the film *I, Daniel Blake*. Of course, those decision makers follow rules, but these are very complex, and the decision maker must decide how they apply to the present case. So, though decision makers try not to act arbitrarily, it can feel to the claimant like they are subject to the arbitrary will of another person. This is unpleasant for the petitioner, but also for the poor employee of the Department for Work and Pensions who ends up turning people's lives inside out. These two citizens do not meet on terms of equal freedom. This is to the detriment of them both: they cannot, as the political philosopher, Philip Pettit, puts it, comfortably 'look one another in the eye'.[16]

Conditional benefits also generate dominating relationships in other ways. Because people are uncertain about the amount of available public support, and averse to that uncertainty, they stay on in jobs that, by their better judgement, they would prefer to not stay in. This is bad for their health because of the stress of being dominated within those jobs. It is also bad for the labour market. Classical economic models of the labour market assume it to be efficient, in that everyone ends up working as much as they want at the things they think they are good at and enjoy, all the work gets done, and labour is recompensed at its actual economic value. But these models only work if the workers can switch jobs easily. This is part of what gives people their market power, driving up wages and conditions in their sector to be good enough to make the job worth doing (their ability to organise and bargain collectively is the other part of their power). We know in practice that the labour market is more 'sticky' than the models suggest it should be:[17] people stay on in jobs that are unsatisfactory, humiliating or inefficient. The uncertainty introduced by a bad safety net does not make work better, as proponents of welfare retrenchment seem to think. It makes work worse, because people stick in bad jobs that make them sick. If the welfare system took the uncertainty away from switching or retraining, people could do so more easily; employers would have to offer fair conditions to attract genuinely free employees; workplaces would become more sane and attractive; and better, healthier work could get done. You can even make parallel arguments about personal relationships: the uncertainty around social support entitlement has kept many a person in a dominating and damaging relationship.

## Why basic income reduces uncertainty and decreases stress

An important effect of basic income is, for most people, to rebalance the relative sizes of the certain and uncertain parts of their income streams. Basic income is about as certain as any income stream could be, because it does not vary depending on what happens elsewhere in your life; no one can take it away from you as long as you are a legal long-term resident; and the only way it changes is through periodic up-ratings made by a democratically accountable government. The saying goes that the only certain things in life are death and taxes. (The saying is famously attributed to Benjamin Franklin, but seems to come from an early 18th-century play, *The Cobler of Preston*, by Christopher Bullock.) We advocate a world where three things are certain: death, taxes and basic income. We call that progress.

In our conversations in Jarrow, people spontaneously linked uncertainty with stress, and saw the benefit of basic income in reducing both: '[I] think it's the stress of not knowing, like not being able to put food on the table, like you'll have money to like to fall back on. That stress would be gone pretty much instantly with a [basic income].' One participant had to manage five different, zero-hours contracts just to get by, with no regular certainty either about the work on offer in any given week or the income that this would provide. Basic income, on the other hand, would provide them with a stress-reducing material floor on which to stand.

As we saw in Chapter 2, our basic income schemes increase household income for some but not all households. For almost all households, they increase the size of the certain portion of the income stream relative to the uncertain portion. Consider someone currently in gig work, on the edge of benefits system eligibility. We have already seen how they face a double uncertainty: the uncertainty of their paid gigs, and the uncertainty generated by moving in and out of Universal Credit eligibility. Under basic income, there would be no uncertainty at all in the basic income part of their income stream, so they face only one of their current sources of uncertainty. Now consider someone relatively high in the income distribution, but not at the very top. Basic income would be neutral for them in terms of what they bring home in a year: their basic income would come in, but their income tax bill might go up. However, the basic income part is entirely certain. We have in effect moved part of their income stream from the uncertain component to the certain component, not changing its average size, but changing its average certainty. Finally consider someone at the very top of the income distribution. They could well be a net payer-in under our schemes. But, they do get something out of their net contribution, as well as knowing they are helping other members of society. They get the best form of insurance possible: even if things go catastrophically worse for them than at present, they are insured against complete ruin, with an insurance that pays out unconditionally and immediately. As we move towards schemes 2 and 3, the insurance is generous enough to make life liveable even in the worst of times, with less and less need for the government to provide additional, conditional, uncertain forms of assistance.

This discussion of uncertainty gives us some perspective on why basic income was not introduced in prior reforms of the UK welfare state. In effect, the forms and magnitudes of uncertainty that people experienced in earlier decades were different. As long as people of working age (in fact, mainly men, at the time) were healthy and could get jobs, then their incomes were fairly steady and their ability to feed their families was not much in doubt. They needed to be protected from two chief risks: work-impairing illness or accident, and cyclical unemployment. These were rare, easy to detect events that could be handled somewhat satisfactorily by assessment once the need arose. This is a very different situation from the current one, where household composition is more fluid; job tenure is shorter; and many people rely on a mosaic of variable income sources. Basic income seems particularly suited to this situation, in which the uncertainty on the part of eligibility assessors is nearly as high as the uncertainty on the part of those in need of assistance.

By reducing the uncertainty (and domination) that we all experience, basic income will reduce our stress. This will produce a physical and mental health dividend that is perhaps larger than that due to the distributional effect of the policy alone. The figures on the population impact of our basic income schemes in Chapter 2 incorporated only the predicted health gains in the lower part of the income distribution due to raising income. This probably underestimates the total benefit: the certainty dividend could be even larger, and, importantly, it will accrue to a larger segment of the population.

The breadth of the class of net beneficiaries is important in terms of building a political coalition for the introduction of the policy, an issue to which we return in Chapter 7. Most people have the intuition that the worst off in society should be helped.[18] This intuition does not seem to be reducible to some kind of veiled self-interest. Nonetheless, it certainly helps the palatability of the policy if the size of the group that benefits directly and demonstrably is large. This chapter has argued that we *all* gain from basic income. Reducing stress is a benefit we can all relate to and almost all of us would feel. It is thus a helpful one to emphasise in making the political case.[19]

**Case Study: Uncertainty and stress in Newcastle**

In Newcastle upon Tyne, the city council, and their partners in the organisation Children and Families Newcastle, see how financial insecurity drives people into increasing debt, isolation, stress and coercion. In Newcastle, 28 per cent of households are in the bottom 10 per cent of incomes nationally[20] and nearly three in ten children live in low-income families.[21]

Beneath these statistics lie stories of how uncertainty generates stress. Sally Noden, from Action for Children, manages services that reach some of the lowest-income families in the city. Sally tells us that 'those with very low household incomes experience impossible stresses. A lack of income means lack of resources and choices, and under that pressure, problems can develop quickly'. In these vulnerable situations, exploitation and control can become a dysfunctional reality. This is especially the case for women who experience financial abuse, where lack of resources and choices leave women exposed to having their resources controlled, prevented from seeking work (or conversely, pressured into working multiple low-paid jobs), having debts racked up in their name, or being forced into being dependent on an abusive partner who controls their finances. These experiences of vulnerability are the bases for domination. Basic income is the remedy, enabling us to escape from the fear of destitution and the constraints it imposes on our opportunities, changing all those stories behind the statistics.

4

# Changing behaviour and strengthening communities

We hear a lot about the behaviour of individuals who face situations of poverty and adversity – too much, probably. They don't plan for the future; they don't budget; they don't form stable marriages; they smoke; they are careless and spendthrift; they are antisocial. These sweeping generalisations are invoked as explanations for individual poverty and the problems of deprived communities. This makes it seem like the problem of poverty is one of individual psychology: if you could change the way individuals think and behave, you would reduce poverty and the societal ills it leads to.

The authors of this book largely reject this explanatory lens. In affluent market societies, the most salient driving causes of poverty are government policies. The driving causes of government policies are complex: what gets enacted depends on who holds power, which interest groups they represent, how political bargaining processes work out, but also on what kinds of arguments can be made persuasively enough in the public forum to get people to talk about them. That is why we are writing this book.

The case that government policies are the most relevant frame for understanding the causes of poverty has been persuasively made by the political scientist, David Brady.[1] For example, when governments are elected for whom reducing poverty and inequality are committed goals, poverty falls sharply. When governments are elected whose priority is to allow the holders of capital to accumulate more capital, that happens, and the rate of poverty goes up. The factors cited by people who advocate individual behavioural explanations, like the rates of young motherhood or single motherhood, are *correlated* with poverty within a population at any one time, but they don't lead the change to a different poverty regime. Government policies do.

This implies, by the way, that the modern state is actually a very effective institution: not perfect, perhaps, but capable of bringing about historic, life-changing social progress, or of undoing it. In this book, we have seen multiple lines of evidence that this is so. As well as Brady's work, there is the work of Clare Bambra cited in Chapter 2: when governments are in power that pursue the goals of redistribution, better access to healthcare and political inclusion, the health of the worst off in society improves rapidly.[2] There is also the work by Lucia Macchia and Andrew Oswald, cited in Chapter 3: government social spending is an effective way of relieving the level of worry in a population, and reducing such spending is an effective way of making worry go up.[3] The fact that the state is such an effective and consequential organisation means it is worth engaging with it, not to roll it back but to make it better. We should care who runs it, how, and in whose interest. It also means that trying to reform the decision making of individuals is a hopeless level at which to intervene on poverty and inequality, like trying to prevent climate change by relocating individual polar bears.

Nonetheless, the proponents of individual behavioural explanations do get something right. There are certain patterns of thought and behaviour that are more prevalent in contexts of poverty and deprivation. People facing these challenges tend to adopt more short-term perspectives, and often make different decisions regarding risks. We don't think of these tendencies as the primary causes of their poverty and deprivation, or even as necessarily irrational. People are put into material situations where these are the decisions that make the best sense under the circumstances. However, the decisions still have downsides, both for the individuals themselves and for society. If, through institutional reform, we can reduce the prevalence of poverty and deprivation, then people are less often put into positions in which they need to make short-termist and risky decisions. This will generate a payoff to them, and also to those around them. In short, if we reduce poverty and deprivation, we will see two payoffs for the health and wellbeing of the population. The primary payoff is the direct improvement from the reduction in the direct effect of scarcity and stress. The second payoff, like an echo, comes about as people become able to take longer-term and more fruitful decisions about their individual health and wellbeing and those of others around them. This echoing, twice-beneficial effect was dubbed by Gillian Pepper the *double dividend* of safety.[4] Make people's worlds safer, and not only are they better off, they have reasons to make themselves better off still.

We believe that the introduction of basic income would generate a double dividend. This double dividend would lead to more health-protecting behaviour; greater sociality and caring; reductions in crime; greater productivity; and more innovation. The simulations we have described in Chapter 2 about the effects of basic income only modelled some of the *static effects* on health and wealth: the effects based on assuming that everyone's situation would remain the same other than having their basic income and possibly paying different rates of tax. But there are also far-reaching *dynamic* consequences of the policy, consequences due to people changing their behaviour and outlook once they know their basic income is there. These dynamic effects are hard to model, but we can make plausible arguments about some of the ways they would look. They are potentially more important than the static effects in the long run.

### Time horizons and the double dividend

Perhaps the best documented finding in the psychology of poverty is that those of us facing poverty focus more on the short term compared to those of us enjoying affluence.[5] This manifests in a relative neglect of or underinvestment in expenditures that will pay off only in the far future. By expenditures, we mean literal expenditures, like putting money into savings or pension investments or subscriptions or training, but also expenditures in a more metaphorical sense, like forgoing the pleasure and boost of nicotine now because you know it will make you healthier later, or going for health checkups and following preventative health advice when you are well.

Prior to the pandemic, we carried out research among general practitioners (GPs) working in areas of deprivation in Northeast England.[6] These doctors had noticed exactly this disengagement from long-term health outcomes among their patients:

> [Our] patients tend to see their long-term chronic conditions as far less important than their more pressing and immediate health needs, such as lack of income, risk of losing their homes, chaotic family situations and low mood. They are unlikely to prioritise quitting smoking, reducing their alcohol intake, improving their diet, and other risk factor management over issues which have a palpable impact on their current quality of life.

Focusing on shorter-term payoffs when resources are scarce is a comprehensible response to scarcity and deprivation, for two non-exclusive reasons.[7] The first of these is obvious: there are needs that must be satisfied now, and you can only begin to spend on investments that pay off in the future once the pressing current needs are made good. You can't eat next year; you need to eat today, and every day. You can't tell your landlord that you will pay them a load of rent once you've invested in the stock market. So, the ability to make financial investments that are future-oriented only really becomes a possibility if there is a surplus of money above present, non-deferrable basic needs. You can also apply this explanation in terms of mental energy. There are times when it is psychologically taxing enough just to navigate through today, and there is no mental bandwidth left for solving future problems.

The second explanation is in terms of *collection risk*. An investment in the future is never absolutely certain to pay off. We could put money in an account with a nice rate of interest, but the bank could collapse before we take it out again. We could carefully avoid tobacco and follow health advice, and be hit by falling debris from an airliner flying overhead anyway. The level of concern about the future that it makes sense to have is affected by the level of collection risk. You really don't worry about your retirement plan when there is fighting raging around you. Those of us living in poverty and deprivation might experience increased levels of collection risk in various ways. We are more exposed to eviction, social instability, pollution, unsafe roads, unsafe workplaces and random violence, all of which could jeopardise our return on thinking about the long future. Those of us in poverty typically judge that we are less in control of the outcomes that matter to us; and, rationally, we may well be right.[8] In short, facing poverty and insecurity, we often *cannot* make investments in the distant future, because we don't have the resource; and sometimes it *would not make sense* for us to do so, even if we could, because the future reward might not turn up, or we would not be around to benefit from it.

We can now explain the idea of the double dividend more concretely. Imagine a world where people have only just enough money to keep their bicycles on the road, and the rate of bicycle theft is quite high. In this world, there is a costly treatment – rust prevention, say – that people can apply to prolong the life of their bike in the future. Do they apply it? Or course not. They haven't the money to spare, and moreover their bike is quite likely to get stolen before they reap the benefit. Now, we give the bike owners extra resource, and suppress bike theft. What is the effect on the longevity of their bikes? There is a primary effect – they have their bikes for a bit longer on average because those bikes are less likely to get stolen. And there is a secondary effect: now they apply the rust treatment too, because they have the resources to invest in it and it is worth their while. This increases the longevity of their bikes a bit more still. The double dividend. Because of our intervention, they could actually spend less on replacing bikes in the very long run.

The claim that basic income would produce a double dividend in this way is a conjecture on our part. The double dividend is a fairly new idea, it has not exactly been tested in randomised control trials. Nonetheless, there is circumstantial evidence that double dividend effects occur, and the case that basic income would produce one is plausible. First, and especially as we move towards schemes 2 and 3 and the minimum income standard, basic income would ensure that people always have the resources to defray their immediate basic needs. They could then devote some of their additional income to projects that constitute investments in their futures. Everyone would be able to adopt the mindset that the comfortable professional classes have the luxury of adopting now, should they wish to. Second, the general collection risks of the environment would go down. This would be for several reasons. People would have the resources and psychological bandwidth to mitigate the hazards that are most salient to them. The people around them would also be getting basic income (with certainty, for ever), and therefore would start to behave in different ways, thinking about *their* futures and avoiding certain kinds of desperate risk. That would make the whole social environment less harsh and more predictable.

Some evidence that unconditional cash increases long-term thinking comes from a remarkable natural experiment in the Eastern Cherokee band of Native Americans. In the 1990s, a casino was introduced on their reservation land (because Native American land is exempt from some anti-gambling laws). Half of the revenues were earmarked for distribution as an unconditional cash transfer to all community members. This adds up to several thousand dollars per person per year, and poverty rates have plummeted. A recent study examined the effect of receiving the cash transfer on young people's projections of how long they thought they were going to live.[9] To do this, the researchers had both to compare Eastern Cherokee respondents over time, in order to see what happened as the cash payments ramped up; and benchmark this against non-Cherokee residents of the local area, who were not eligible for the payments, and so would not be affected by their introduction. There was a staggering 15-year increase in subjective life expectancy in the Eastern Cherokee men. People's perceptions of how long they will live are somewhat related to how long they actually do live; but the real significance of the subjective variable is that it tells you a lot about how people feel about their futures. If they feel they are going die young anyway, there seems limited incentive to make longer-term investments and choices. To be long-termist, they have to feel like there is a long term. The increase in subjective life expectancy was restricted to the men; young Eastern Cherokee women did not see a corresponding increase. The reason for this is not clear, but given how much social trouble (crime, violence, and so on) is driven by 'young male syndrome', the large increase in young men's appraisals that they have a future is surely noteworthy.

We have stressed that we do not see basic income as the only way the state should reduce uncertainty and collection risk. It also needs to provide basic services and ensure safety standards and protections. But basic income is a very fundamental way of making the world safer. It is also a relatively non-paternalistic one. It trusts people to know what investments they want to make in their own future, and resources them to make the decisions they need to make to give themselves futures worth investing for, by their own lights. In other words, in a world of basic income, not only do you get the direct payoff of the relief of the suffering and stresses of poverty, we predict that we would start to see more rapid declines in smoking, better diets, more savings for the future, and greater interest in health and wellbeing into older age. There is evidence from epidemiology, experimental psychology and cash transfer trials that supports the plausibility of such shifts. Moreover, our Jarrow participants intuited that these shifts would take place, too:

> Maybe the reason why we find it difficult to eat healthy or to exercise or to find the things that we enjoy doing is partly because our brains are changed because of the stress that we're under ... so I wonder whether actually just having a different system where we have that money, would mean we were under less stress and have more chance [to do so].

### Taking risks and the cliff of desperation

In life, there are risks that it would be good for people to take, but sometimes they don't; and risks that it is really bad for people to take, but sometimes they do anyway. (In this section, when we talk about risks, we mean decisions that could have good consequences, or could have bad ones; this is a slightly different sense of risk than in 'health risk' or 'collection risk'.) Good risks are those which, on average, are going to improve people's wellbeing and not damage the wellbeing of anyone around. For example, a person might have a great idea for a new business venture, or have a hunch that they would do really well in a different profession. In both these cases, there is a chance it goes badly (the new business fails, the other profession turns out to be saturated), and so it is risky. Nonetheless, there is a decent chance it would go very well. We want to live in a society where people can take these good risks: they make people feel fulfilled and generate economic and cultural dynamism.

Bad risks are risks that just might lead to some gain, but on average leave the person themselves, and usually other people as well, worse off. For example, I might steal a loaf of bread or a packet of nappies. This might well get me a loaf of bread or a packet of nappies; but there is a real chance it would leave me with a hefty fine and a criminal record. That outcome would be so incredibly costly that it makes no sense for me to take the chance. Indeed, that is why society has set those penalties so high: to make it not worth taking the chance. This is a bad risk even from the very narrow perspective of someone who wants a loaf of bread or a packet of nappies, before we even come to the broader costs to society. We want to make a world where no one feels tempted to take these bad risks.

Poverty has what is referred to as a Manichean effect on risk taking: those of us in poverty are often among the most risk-averse in society and *also* make up the bulk of those who take the most extreme risks.[10] Indeed, the tragedy of poverty is that people often can't afford to take good risks (which, on average, would make their lives better), but are occasionally strongly tempted to take very bad risks (which, on average, make their lives worse). A theory to explain this complex effect of poverty on risk taking is the *desperation threshold model*.[11]

According to the desperation threshold model, the satisfaction of human needs in any given society has a somewhat cliff-faced shape. If you have a place to live, enough to eat and what political philosopher John Rawls called 'the social basis of respect', then your life may not be perfect, but you are managing. Things could be a lot worse. You are on the top of the cliff. On the other hand, once you no longer have enough money to hold on to a place to live, and you can't put food on the table, you have fallen off the cliff. The financial difference between the person who is atop the cliff and the person who has fallen off might only be a few pounds, but the difference between their lives is catastrophic. If you are off the cliff, it is an emergency. You cannot just keep your head down. You need to do something.

The idea of the desperation threshold allows us to make sense of the effects of poverty on risk taking. Most of us in poverty are currently on top of the cliff, but not far from the edge. This affects our decision making when we are offered a good risk, like a business idea or the possibility of retraining. If the good risk works out well, we will move considerably further inland, away from the cliff. And it probably will work out well. However, there is a small chance that it goes wrong in some way: that is what makes it a risk. In this event, we will move backwards, towards the cliff. Those who are affluent can take these kinds of risks whenever they want. They know that even if things run against them on this occasion, they are so far from the cliff that the misfortune of their venture going awry would not take them over; and they might learn something from the attempt. For those of us in poverty, the venture going wrong would be enough to take us over the edge, and this is not something we can countenance. Thus, under these circumstances, we constantly have to forgo options that would make our lives richer and would on average improve our state, because we simply can't expose ourselves to a non-zero chance of falling to ruin.

On the other hand, when exposed to poverty, particularly in countries like the UK marked by high inequality and inadequate social protections, people do fall down the cliff at a certain rate. It is a small minority of all the people in poverty, but it does happen. Once we have fallen down the cliff, all the calculus around risks is flipped. We no longer care about the fact that risks might send us over the edge: that has already happened. At this point, we simply cannot remain where we are. We need to take any option, however hare-brained, that has some chance of getting us back above the cliff edge. If it goes wrong, well, things can hardly be worse. Social scientist Benoît de Courson compares this situation to a football team losing a crucial match by one goal, with five minutes to play. The goalkeeper leaves the goal and tries to score at the other end. The most likely consequence is that the team concedes another goal, since they have no functioning goalkeeper. But they are about to lose anyway: losing by two goals is scarcely worse than losing by one. And there is a one in a thousand chance that the goalkeeper equalises by scoring in the other goal or helps the team in scoring. In other words, in the last five minutes when losing anyway, the team has an incentive to take a really bad risk, because they are already at rock bottom.

We've long recognised that poverty drives people to take bad risks in this way. It is the story of Jean Valjean in Victor Hugo's *Les Misérables*, driven by the moral coercion of want to steal a loaf of bread to feed his family, despite the immense penalty this carried. Small crimes of acquisition are disproportionately committed by people with very low levels of material resources, and are more frequent where inequality is high, when unemployment increases and when incomes at the bottom of the distribution are squeezed.[12] The perpetrators don't exactly have a preference for committing these crimes, or think they are a good idea, but they feel desperate for a way of generating fast cash, to deal with a crisis.[13] In taking their desperate risks, they imperil their own livelihoods and make things less pleasant and more unpredictable for everybody else.

Imagine a Britain under scheme 3, or at least scheme 2, of our basic income schemes. Not only are people's basic needs then met, but they can know that those needs will always be met in the future, however the chips land. In such a case, the prudential reason for not taking a risk you see as a good one is never very salient. You know, in effect, that you will be protected from falling down the cliff in the worst case. On the other hand, there should be vanishingly few people who are ever below the cliff, at least for economic reasons. A central type of situation that motivates people to take desperate, bad risks, should hardly ever occur. This would not only reduce the crime rate, but have a spreading positive effect on social relations in general. Crime drives fear, withdrawal and distrust of others. Knowing that other people are not now, and will not in future be, desperate propagates reassuring signals of social possibility throughout the whole population.

## The double dividend for communities

So far in this chapter, we have proposed a double dividend from the introduction of basic income in terms of individual health, prudence and wellbeing. People don't have to forgo good risks for fear of falling, and don't have to take bad risks in desperation. They have the resource to invest for the future, and collection risk goes down as individuals behave more predictably and can avoid outcomes like eviction. Thus, they look after their long-term interests.

We also see the double dividend as applying above and beyond individual outcomes. There is a double dividend for communities, too. The kinds of behaviours that make communities work well as a whole often require that individuals composing them are secure and are taking a long-term view. Think of community service; of getting involved in local politics; of volunteering; of holding the powerful to account; of improving our local environments; or of just upholding simple norms of civility. These simple social goods all depend on the presence of what Guy Standing dubbed 'the shadow of the future', the reasonable expectation that the community and one's place in it are somewhat durable and predictable stretching forwards in time.[14] When there is a shadow of the future, these social goods become not just possible, but attractive as ways to invest time and effort. Economic precarity erodes the shadow of the future; basic income would restore it. Although our focus and justification in this book is often in terms of the health of individuals, we do not want to neglect the broader harvest in terms of community health and wellbeing that basic income could bring. Figure 1.1 captures these community level payoffs, partly and perhaps inadequately, in the band towards the middle, of 'indirect socioeconomic impacts'.

For our Jarrow participants, it was the community-level double dividend that was the most inspiring potential consequence of introducing a basic income. Participants linked material scarcity and insecurity to a perceived erosion of community activity at present. Parents pointed to the increased time they would spend caring for their children and the wellbeing benefits that all would enjoy as a result. One participant said that people would not have to shoplift if they had more money, potentially freeing up police time for other priorities. Others went further, arguing that basic income would liberate people's 'contribution energy' and free them and the community as a whole to engage in life-affirming, communal activities:

> I do think that [by] having this extra money there's going to be pros and cons … but I think some of the pros we're talking about relate to poverty. Like, if you've got extra money, you maybe wouldn't have to be working all hours, like carers, having to work all hours under the sun. You could have extra time where you could do community-based things, like … community allotments, where you grow your own food amongst the community, share amongst the community, educate each other about things like 'You don't have to be taking drugs, you can take your mind off things in other ways.'

This view was echoed:

> I think the [basic income], it's going to free up people's time a little bit, to do other things to help each other. Like I said before, if you're not working 16 hours a day and sleeping for four hours, you've got that extra money where you can contribute to helping be a community again and caring about each other again, and it doesn't just necessarily have to just be just Jarrow, care about society as a whole.

Other members of this group concurred, and the conversation ranged for ten minutes over how community life might flourish again once the 'better angels of our human nature', as one man put it, had time and space to take flight. Community-level health feeds back into individual health in a virtuous spiral. There is nothing more salutary for humans, who we have known since Aristotle to be animals adapted to society, than to be integrated into a society that is functioning well, because everyone has contribution energy.

## Case Study: The social basis of dysfunction

The image of antisocial behaviour being the cause rather than symptom of deprivation is deeply flawed, and obscures the impact of instability, lack of opportunity and long-term insecurity.[15] Community groups in Jarrow know this too well. Roweena Russell of Big Local Jarrow, puts this plainly: 'People in Jarrow are resourceful, hardworking and proud, but for an important minority of families we see the pressures that come with low income result in things coming apart at the seams.'

Jarrow's rate of 153 crimes per 1,000 people is 39 per cent higher than average rates in Tyne and Wear.[16] It has led to such news reports as 'Feral teens in masks terrorising communities'[17] and Jarrow's Neighbourhood Policing Team focusing on resident concerns about drug dealing, antisocial behaviour and criminal damage.[18]

Behind these headlines, the forces really driving antisocial behaviour and addiction are generally overlooked. Russell explains that:

> When you have few options, few resources that are yours and little to lose, focusing on the long-term is not straightforward. It's easy to judge, but the pressure some of our poorest households face is terrible and we need to remember that, if we were to find ourselves in these circumstances, our behaviour might not be that different. It's the deprivation that's the biggest crime here.

Low income is a toxic risk factor. When combined with limited opportunities, underfunded services and social strain, things can go badly wrong. As Russell concludes, the introduction of basic income is the foundation stone in addressing these ills.

> What potential is lost when people don't have enough. What might schools do if every child had enough? What might happen in our society if everyone had enough? We've become austerity hardwired and don't even comment on that fact that no public service in England works because so many have so little. For those concerned by good use of public spending, this should be the first consideration. What could we do if everyone was alright? Perhaps we have to be really brave to find out.

5

# Care across generations

A functioning society involves the provision of care, on a massive scale. Children are cared for by parents, and others. At the other end of life, senior citizens are cared for by their friends, relatives and others. People with serious illnesses are cared for by their friends, families and others. This means that over the course of life, a typical person will find themselves needing care at some points, and also wishing to provide care to others at some points. We provide care in a hybrid way. On the one hand, there are professional carers, for whom it is paid work. On the other, there is the much larger load of unpaid care that people wish to provide informally for their loved ones. The state recognises that care needs to be paid for. In some cases, it supports people who provide unpaid care financially (for example, through Carer's Allowance). This recognises, in effect, that the state would need to pay for the care if it were not being provided informally. On the other hand, adults get no specific incentive for deciding to care for their own children. Instead, they get a free childcare allowance, tax breaks and (if their incomes are low enough) refunds of further childcare costs through Universal Credit, to pay someone else to do it, but nothing if they choose to do it themselves.

In short, as elsewhere, the current system is an incoherent patchwork that sets up perverse incentives. In some cases, people can get a payment from the government to provide informal care; but of course this payment is conditional, and hence will be withdrawn if the person's situation improves slightly, or docked if the carer finds time to do a bit of paid work as well. In other cases, the state would pay for your neighbour to look after your kids, and you to look after theirs, but not for you to choose to look after your own. Meanwhile those who provide care for a living, who often do so by vocation, are so low-paid and hard-stretched that they are very challenged to do their jobs as well as they would like. It is desperately important for society that the work of caring gets done, and done well. In an ideal system, people would have more meaningful freedom to choose between providing care themselves and procuring paid care. They would be adequately supported in either case, and they would be able to mix and move between paid work and caring without penalty. You will already have guessed what our claim will be: basic income would help us move closer to this ideal situation.

### The importance of childhood

Compared to other countries, the children in the UK get off to a poor start. We come in at 35th in the world for infant mortality,[1] and while the rate has come down over time, other countries have seen a faster decline. We are losing ground compared to other nations. When comparing purely to 38 other rich OECD and European Union countries, we come in at 29th for child mental wellbeing, 19th for child physical health and 26th for skills.[2] Meanwhile, out of 33 countries, the UK is ranked 31st, only above Japan and Turkey, for life satisfaction at age 15. Worryingly, young people in the UK are also increasingly likely to be disabled, with the percentage rising from 7 per cent as recently as 2015/2016 to 11 per cent in 2022/2023.[3] This is a similar percentage-point increase as among working-age people over the same period (18 per cent to 23 per cent), while the rate for people of state pension age has stayed broadly flat (44 per cent to 45 per cent). Issues that we previously believed would only emerge in later life are emerging far earlier.

In 2022/2023, children in the UK had a 30 per cent chance of living in poverty after housing costs.[4] The Resolution Foundation estimated in January 2023 that the rate will increase to 32.5 per cent in 2027/2028, the worst since 1998/1999.[5] By that time, the analysis suggests that 55 per cent of children in families with three or more children will be in poverty, while the figure for families of four or more will be 77 per cent. This is, in large part, due to the two-child benefits limit, which restricts additional Universal Credit payments for children to the first two in a family.[6] Nine parliamentary constituencies had child poverty rates above 50 per cent in 2021/2022, with Birmingham hosting the top three (and four overall), while Greater Manchester has another three. Housing costs have a devastating impact in some areas, with London local authorities and constituencies each containing the 20 worst in terms of percentage point difference in poverty rates before and after housing costs. In West Ham, 23 per cent of children are counted as being in poverty before housing costs, but after housing costs this shoots up to 47.5 per cent. The Northeast has particularly suffered over time, with a 33.8 per cent increase in child poverty between 2014/2015 and 2021/2022 and Middlesbrough's rate rising from 29 per cent to 41 per cent, the largest increase of any local authority.

All of this means that there is a very significant chance of being born into poverty in modern Britain, the fifth or sixth largest economy in the world.[7] This sets a child off on a path from which the prospects for escape are bleak: children from poor families have worse outcomes than their wealthy counterparts.[8] In 2014, using data from almost a decade before, a government review found that 50 per cent of the relative difference in parents' incomes was 'transmitted' to their children.[9] And while teenagers experiencing poverty in the mid-1970s were twice as likely to still be in poverty as adults compared to those who had not experienced poverty as children, for teenagers in the mid-1980s, this had doubled to a fourfold increase in risk.

The presumed solution to family poverty has been to encourage parents back into the paid workplace, to boost household income through wages. But this steers from the Scylla of low household incomes straight into the Charybdis of high childcare costs. According to the 2024 Coram Childcare Survey, the average weekly cost in Great Britain of a full-time, 50-hour nursery place for those aged less than two was £302, for two-year-olds was £288 and for those aged three to four was £121 (the latter with 30 hours of free childcare having already been deducted).[10] In Inner London, the figures were far higher, at £428, £431 and £377 respectively. In 2022, the UK had the sixth most expensive net childcare costs of all OECD nations at 25 per cent of the salary of a couple with average earnings.[11] The figure for a couple in Germany, on the other hand, stood at 1 per cent, or in Sweden at 5 per cent.

This crippling cost is affecting a huge proportion of parents. Data from the 2022/2023 Family Resources Survey suggests that 53 per cent of families with children use any form of childcare, with 25 per cent using formal childcare, 12 per cent informal, and 15 per cent both formal and informal. A 2023 study from campaigning charity Pregnant Then Screwed found that 26 per cent of parents who use formal childcare said the cost was more than three-quarters of their disposable income, while 76 per cent of mothers who pay for childcare said the costs were so high that it no longer made sense for them to work.[12] Even following the introduction of 15 hours of free childcare from 1 April 2024, Pregnant Then Screwed found that 25 per cent of parents would save less than £90 per month, that 22 per cent of parents eligible for the support were still considering leaving work or reducing hours and that 62 per cent reported that costs had increased in the previous six months anyway.[13] Universal Credit claimants are eligible each month for up to 85 per cent of their childcare costs, but given that this is only up to £646 for one child and £1,108 for two or more,[14] many find a return even to full-time work unaffordable. In sum: parents face a difficult set of trade-offs. If they decide to do less paid work, to provide quality childcare themselves, household incomes stay low, with all the difficulties that brings; whereas on the other hand if they do more paid work, almost all of the gain – perhaps more – will be eaten up in childcare costs.

For the working-age adults who become professional carers, life can be even more challenging. Full-time care workers in the UK in 2023 had a median gross salary of £23,950, while, including part-time workers, the overall figure was just £18,577.[15] Given that the relative poverty threshold before housing costs for a single parent of two children is £363 per week or £18,876 per year,[16] many full-time care workers are likely to be just scraping by. Indeed, analysis undertaken for the Trades Union Congress found that one in four children with a care worker parent are in poverty.[17] This is no surprise, as our analysis of the 2023 Labour Force Survey found that 22.4 per cent of social care workers are lone parents. That compares with 10.4 per cent of employees overall. We are subjecting the people to whom we entrust the care of our family members to poverty wages. Indeed, we are condemning their own children to a much-increased risk of lifetime poverty.

So, in sum, we have a modern society – one of the wealthiest in the world – with going on for a third of children born into poverty, with a system that prevents them from escaping poverty, who then become parents to more children born into poverty and who are unable to be productive or develop the kind of security that is essential to ageing well. This is a waste of life for the individuals and a waste of economic potential for society. It is individual and collective suffering as policy. It is no surprise that birth rates are at their lowest on record, with people in their 30s now much less likely to have children.[18]

## Later life

Even those individuals who are sceptical about basic income would likely agree that those who work for decades are entitled to a secure later life for both them and their families. Unfortunately, the current heavily means-tested and conditional social care system is both poor quality and a burden on the individual, their family and the state. The average weekly cost for residing in a care home is £800 and for those in nursing homes, it's £1,078. Full payment is required of anyone with capital over £23,250 (including their home in many circumstances).[19] Meanwhile, in 2021/2022, average weekly income for pensioner couples was £515 and for single pensioners was £239.[20] There is, just as in early years care, a huge gap between costs and the means of paying for them.

With regard to perverse incentives, as in caring for children, so in caring for aged parents. Carer's Allowance, for example, is both insufficient and full of the kinds of conditionality traps that result in people being forced to repay their entire benefit for engaging with paid work or study alongside their caring. It is, put simply, the absolute worst of all worlds. To receive just £81.90 per week for at least 35 hours of otherwise unpaid care, carers cannot study for more than 21 hours per week, and cannot earn a penny more than £151 per week after tax, National Insurance and allowed expenses.[21] To put this into perspective, a member of the House of Lords can claim a flat-rate payment of £361 in expenses for declaring a single day of attendance at Westminster.[22]

This strict conditionality means that informal carers who are effectively paid way under the National Living Wage for the care they provide, are being sent demands to repay up to £20,000 and being criminally prosecuted. Media reports suggest that this is the result of years-long delays in identifying 'overpayment', due to ministers only providing sufficient resourcing to check half of the overpayment alerts it received from technology it put into place in 2018.[23] The issue, now being widely reported as the 'Carer's Allowance scandal',[24] was highlighted by the National Audit Office, the government's spending watchdog, in 2019 and was clearly not dealt with in the entire subsequent parliamentary term. The National Audit Office decided to investigate, again, in 2024.[25] This Kafkaesque bureaucracy affects everyone involved in such fragile care relationships. An 85-year-old woman with dementia, heart failure and kidney disease, for example, was ordered to repay £13,000. In her case, this is the delayed result of her son taking on full-time caring for her in 2019 and therefore receiving £50 per week carer's element within Universal Credit. This meant she was no longer eligible for the severe disability premium of her pension credit.[26] The Department for Work and Pensions took some five years to identify the issue despite administering the benefits of both mother and son. If the very organisation responsible for delivering such benefits takes half a decade to follow up, how can we expect individuals, often in very vulnerable circumstances and who are unlikely to understand the complex web of rules, to do so? Indeed, the government has apologised for a similar case and written off the debt, though it appears solely because the claimant had dementia and therefore could not be expected to inform the authorities of the change in circumstances.[27] Yet it has failed to take action to address the systemic dysfunction, instead focusing simply on the individual symptoms of it.

Conditional systems of support always leave room for these kinds of devastating eligibility problems to occur. It is worse than that: in conditional systems, governments are often looking to reduce the number of claimants, and so they more or less deliberately create a 'hostile environment' for anyone who might be eligible. Disabled people feel the brunt of this throughout their lives. For example, disabled people fear being physically active in case they lose disability benefits that support that activity in the first place.[28] But as we see in the case of disability benefits, this kind of conditionality does nothing to achieve the objectives set out by successive governments, including reducing the caseload and focusing support 'on those who need it most'. Governments from (at the very least) New Labour onwards have been promising to end 'sicknote culture' and 'focus on what people can do rather than what they can't'.[29] But this never works and never will: it is intervention in the wrong place.

Despite the hostile environment, the number of disabled people has increased, the number claiming sickness and disability benefits has increased, and outcomes have continued to get worse.[30] Conditionality does nothing other than creating disincentives to managing impairments and health conditions, being economically active and undertaking care for our families and our communities. This is socially corrosive, harmful to families and devastating to the nation's health. Fifty-eight per cent of people aged 80 and above are disabled according to 2020/2021–2022/2023 Family Resources Survey data.[31] Data from the 2021 Census shows that 16 per cent of people aged 50–64 in England provide some amount of unpaid care, including 19 per cent, almost one in five, of women in that age group.[32] With an ever-increasing number of disabled children and working-age people, as well as an ageing population, the need for care is likely to permeate an ever-greater proportion of our lives.

## How would basic income improve the problems of caring?

Basic income cannot resolve all the issues around the need for care, and its costs, immediately or in full. More comprehensive reform is essential, including childhood and adult social care services free at the point of use.[33] We can only take advantage of efficiencies of scale if we have nationalised systems with consistent, predictable funding, that will repay itself in improved educational and economic outcomes that will emerge over time.

Basic income does, however, have two sets of very positive effects. For families, it makes a lot of the dilemmas around integrating paid work with care for loved ones much simpler. It sweeps away the web of bureaucracy, complexity and perverse incentives, leaving parents freer to choose what's best for them, in their own circumstances, between looking after kids and/or returning to paid employment. At the moment, because Universal Credit is conditional, and provides some allowance for paid care, there are high marginal deduction rates for parents making decisions about the trade-off between paid work and parenting; even at times financial incentives to dissolve households. Basic income, on the other hand, will be predictably there whatever decisions they make.

With a basic income, a parent could opt to stay at home and receive enough income to have some financial independence and give their children the kind of care that results in long-term societal benefit. On the other hand, they, or their partners, would not face such high marginal deduction rates when they moved into more paid work. For example, a single parent, currently trapped by childcare costs and benefit conditions, would have the breathing space to begin to make inroads into work when possible, without fearing a bureaucratic nightmare and financial disincentives.

In middle age, basic income would mean that an individual could take time out of work or reduce hours to look after a parent or child when they are unwell. It means that, in one action, we eliminate the Carer's Allowance scandal, enable carers to engage in paid work when the person they care for is in better health, and recognise the important contribution that people undertaking any kind of caring responsibility make to the health and economic wellbeing of the nation. Caring is a prosocial contribution,[34] because it means that families are less under strain, and also that every generation is able to stay healthier and have less recourse to the reactive medical care which costs the National Health Service so much of its current budget.

In later life, a basic income means that everyone receives enough to live on even if they have had to take time out of work earlier in life to care for family. No longer would there be the needless costs of administering a means-tested Pension Credit[35] to make up the difference to a full state pension if an individual's contribution record isn't complete. Basic income would ensure that an individual whose partner was the main breadwinner but can no longer work has security into their own old age.

The second set of positive effects would be in supporting people who make their careers in the provision of care. As we have seen, this sector provides a socially very important function, but its members are low-paid and often under terrible strain. Care workers are exactly in the section of the income distribution whose positions will be most improved by basic income (see Chapter 2). Under basic income, life will be better for those choosing to provide care informally, and also better for those who devote their paid careers to providing care.

Penny-pinching on care doesn't save money in the end. It just saves up problems that we have to respond to with reactive services, putting off additional costs to be paid by future generations of taxpayers. It even causes immediate problems for today's taxpayers. We cannot go on with a system that leaves people in destitution and disincentivises social and economic activity. We need something that supports our caring instincts. This isn't just desirable, it's essential. Having more informal care, for example, grandparents taking care of their grandchildren while the parents work, and children being able to provide the care for their parents in later life that will keep them out of hospital or nursing care is a net benefit for everyone. We are currently cutting off our collective nose to spite our societal face by penalising unpaid carers receiving £50 per week so that the state then has to take on the vast bulk of the £1,000 cost of professional care their loved one will require instead.

Our lives are not always a clean, upward diagonal line of growth and autonomy from childhood to death. Even among people who have advantage growing up, life throws up banana peels to slip on. The COVID-19 pandemic demonstrated that even higher earners are not as secure as they once were. Employers go out of business or cut costs on a relative whim; economic and public health crises transform the job market; and personal or familial health problems can emerge at the most inopportune moments. The more generous the basic income scheme, the greater the social and economic benefit. With a higher payment, we could remove all the disincentives and ensure that people of all ages escape poverty, live good lives and support their families, friends and communities. People want to care for each other, across the generations. We must have policies that support that instinct. Basic income is the first step.

### Case Study: Children in care and a basic income pilot

Although most social care in the UK is provided to older people, social care for children is also a spiralling cost to society. In 2023, over 83,000 children were in care, a 30 per cent increase since 2010 and a 15-year high. The rise in child poverty between 2015 and 2020 led to over 10,000 additional children entering care in England. The cost of this is astronomical – the social cost of adverse outcomes for children who need a social worker is an estimated £23 billion annually. The lifetime social costs per child in care is £1.2 million; that's twice as much as for children who need a social worker but are not in residential care.

The costs of children's social care are an increasingly problematic issue for local authorities – caught in the trap of having to provide statutory care at the expense of being able to invest in effective local support for families in need. Between 2015–2016 and 2021–2022, local authority spending on children's residential care more than doubled. As total spending on children in care increased, total spending on preventive services for children and families fell by about a quarter in real terms over the past decade. Over the same period, cuts to adolescent services totalling £58 million led to more 16–17-year-olds entering care, with placement costs totalling £60 million. Cuts to prevention are clearly a false economy. With many local authorities now at risk of bankruptcy, this is a situation that is going to end in disaster.

The Welsh Government is currently piloting a basic income for all young people leaving care, by providing them with an unconditional basic income of £1,600 every month for a period of two years from their 18th birthday. This bold and courageous social policy was born out of the government's interest in trialling a basic income and their recognition of the unique and significant challenges care leavers face in their transition into adulthood. This is a potentially transformative intervention and a golden opportunity to raise the profile of care leavers' needs, generate good evidence about how to help them overcome the challenges of early adulthood, and contribute to the international evidence base on how to reduce poverty and disadvantage.

The pilot is being evaluated by a research team led by CASCADE, the Children's Social Care Research and Development Centre, at Cardiff University. The evaluation will assess the impact of the pilot on the young people who receive the income, looking at their health, wellbeing, education, employment and more, as well as asking how the basic income is experienced by the young people and the adults supporting them, and whether or not the programme is cost-effective. Findings are expected in 2026 with interim and emerging findings published each year. The first annual report is available already.[36]

We already have many examples of care leavers having new opportunities and choices as a result of this scheme, for example, being able to take driving lessons, buy an instrument for a music course, eat more healthily and, crucially, save money for the future. As one young person, attending college and working a part-time job commented:

> I think 18 is the perfect age to receive this, because you're going into adulthood, you gain the responsibility, and it's good to have that financial support when you turn into an adult, because most care leavers, in their childhood, they never had anything that was completely theirs on their own. That they could control. So, I suppose it helped us with feeling in control, and that.

# 6

# A collective return on investment

We subtitled this book 'The policy that changes everything'. It is time to draw together our arguments about basic income's beneficial effects, zoom out to the scale of society as a whole, and make good on the promise of that subtitle. How exactly does basic income change everything?

We can line up the different effects of basic income according to how easy they are to quantify and predict. At the near end, we have effects that are specifiable in money terms, and for which we already can produce reasonable numerical estimates. In the middle are effects that are in principle specifiable in money terms, but we don't have good estimates yet. And, at the far end, are broader social and cultural consequences that are important, but whose value is difficult to express in pounds and pence.

Starting at the near end, one thing we can calculate fairly precisely is the up-front cost. We have already calculated this for our schemes 1, 2 and 3.[1] Hence we know what tax changes would be necessary to fund these without assuming any savings elsewhere. The schemes would not, however, just be a matter of outlay with no return. We have already estimated that the immediate return, in reduced healthcare and social costs, that comes just from the raising of low incomes, is of the order of £3.87 billion per year for scheme 1, rising to around £20 billion for scheme 3 (Chapter 2).

Then we move to costs that are quantifiable but not yet quantified. There is the reduction in uncertainty, and consequent reduction in stress-related ill health beyond the distributional effect (Chapter 3). We don't know how large this is, but it is plausible that it is larger than the £3.87 billion due to poverty reduction. Then, there is the dynamic effect from changes in behaviour: the double dividend (Chapter 4). Actually, there are numerous double dividends: the double dividend in healthcare expenditure as people look after their long-term health and reduce addiction; the double dividend in the criminal justice system as fewer people commit crimes; and the double dividend to the tax authorities as people move to jobs they like better and are more productive in. There are also the long-term payoffs from children getting a better start in life, and the savings from permitting more people to care for members of their families (Chapter 5). We hope all of these payoffs will be better modelled in the near future. The more of these payoffs we factor into the net cost of introducing basic income, the more doing so seems like an easy choice even from a narrowly financial point of view.

The main point of this chapter, though, is to discuss the broader social and cultural changes that live at the far end of the lineup: those that are valuable, but difficult, even in principle, to quantify. Basic income changes everything in these spheres too, from the kinds of relationships we can have, to the loci of power and authority in our lives, to the collective story we can tell ourselves about who we are. Basic income promises to foster a sense of active agency and empowerment for all of us, reversing decades of loss.

## Neoliberal reforms, welfare retrenchment and the loss of authority

For decades, we have been told that national debt and social dysfunction are the results of socially disruptive groups who are dependent on welfare and incapable of positively engaging in society. This is a feint, drawing attention away from the real political and structural causes. Even now, under a Labour government, there is no clear vision of pathways to better lives; the policies pursued are justified mainly by the lack of alternative. We have reached this position over the course of the Millennial Generation's entire lifespan, but the worst excesses have occurred over the past 15 years.

A dominant argument for why poverty and social problems persist that has been advanced for decades is that they stem from 'big government', over-spending and enabling an ever-expanding welfare system that makes people passive and society inefficient.[2] The remedy on offer has usually been to scale back government's role in the economy and society, reducing public spending and placing responsibility on individual voluntary activity to provide essential services. We saw this, for example, in the policy initiative known as the 'Big Society' of the coalition government of 2010 after the global financial crisis.[3]

What is supposed to replace big government, with its connotations of pre-1989 unreconstituted socialism and failing 1970s corporatism, is presented as a liberating series of independent, spontaneous and consensual civic engagements.[4] By placing emphasis back on individuals to address their own challenges, the coalition government argued that Britain could develop a more dynamic, self-sustaining society.[5] Freed from state nannying, people would be able to exercise agency in pursuing better, healthier lives. Dragged from entitlement to self-responsibility, people would be forced to behave in ways that no longer damaged others.

Though policies like the Big Society are presented as liberating, the true drivers are less public-spirited. For sociologist Ruth Levitas,[6] the Big Society project was part of 'a thirty-year process of redistribution to the rich'. Rather than being 'a necessary response to the economic crisis, [Big Society] constitute[d] a neoliberal shock doctrine, forcing through punitive policies which undermine the collective provision against risk'. The approach was illustrative of broader neoliberal reform processes and welfare retrenchment, already underway in Anglophone countries, that accelerated in the wake of the global financial crisis. That acceleration was achieved, in part, by branding reforms 'austerity' measures, implying a temporariness[7] at odds with the long-term nature of the institutional and distributional changes, which are still with us today.

Neoliberal reforms and welfare retrenchment have often achieved precisely the opposite of the stated aims: they have generated destitution, passivity[8] and dysfunction, particularly in those regions, places and communities with existing vulnerabilities.[9] Far from being enhanced, people's authority to act appears to have reduced, alongside their formal entitlement to social security. Owen Jones' book *Chavs*[10] made clear that previously self-organising communities were being torn asunder, continuing the decline that had been felt since deindustrialisation. Guy Standing's book *The Precariat*[11] emphasised that whatever work which did emerge in the state's wake was inevitably precarious; and the money made from economic activity in these communities would inevitably end up being spent and hoarded elsewhere.

Swathes of communities once rich with active roles, institutions of solidarity and associated identities were now consigned to lives defined by permanent conflict with an increasingly inadequate welfare system.[12] Far from gaining autonomy, people lost a sense of having a sphere of authority; even a sense of what their place in society was. As a young male resident of Ashington noted: '[I am] 26 years old, I'm not quite sure how to describe myself, because I don't really have a position or anything to call mine.'

The effect of this loss of authority and clear position permeates every sphere of our lives. The ritual of giving and receiving tea and biscuits is central to working-class communities in Northeast England. Originating as a workplace tool for sustaining productivity through its combination of sugar and caffeine, tea was drawn into working-class homes as a means of improving dry, unpalatable food, eventually becoming an 'integral part of the social fabric'[13] and achieving the status of a rite of respectability.[14] Any visit by an adult to another adult's house would follow a similar pattern. The visitor would be met by the host at the door, who would permit entry and, often immediately after enquiring as to the visitor's health, forcefully offer tea and biscuits. Providing tea and biscuits is a form of authority: the authority of the host to guide guests spatially into their territory, to direct them to sitting spaces and to determine the point at which tea and biscuits are offered. This is their space and, in this space, they have the authority to exercise power. The gift of tea and biscuits is, actually, an assertion of authority and its exercise, an act of social power.

The authority to give, in other words, expresses the social basis of respect, and allows the giver to look the receiver in the eye. The dance of offering to pay for rounds of drinks or meals or other collective expenses is instructive.

The example from *Father Ted* of Mrs Doyle and Mrs Dunne fighting over a bill[15] chimes with generations of people in the Northeast: each opportunity to pay accompanied by a desperate, exaggerated battle to adopt full responsibility for payment. The younger or lower-income party will often strike first, making a gesture that everybody understands to be ridiculous to settle a bill. The older or higher-income party will then call out the madness and move towards the till or waiter with payment in hand. The junior party will then knock back the payment and stand proudly assuming all responsibility before the person awaiting payment. The senior party will respond, assuring the member of staff that they are actually the responsible adult. The junior party will then make a final and extraordinary attempt to throw cash or card at the till or swipe machine, before generally the senior party intervenes, plucks the junior party out of the way and pays. This is all in the name of generosity. But it is not generosity. Or, if it is generosity we ought to view it in a much less gentle light, since this is the active struggle of individuals to sustain authority. Nobody necessarily wants to pay for the sake of paying – who would want to have less money? People want to assume the authority and social agency that goes with payment, or appearing desperate to make payment, often, literally, at great cost. As sociologist Marcel Mauss put it, 'To refrain from giving, just as to refrain from accepting, is to lose rank – as is refraining from reciprocating'.[16] People in Northeast communities understood this well.

Recent research in the region has showed a change.[17] Adults seem to have become resigned to being seen as passive subjects. This reflects the death of a key element of resistance in the deep history of people in the Northeast, since the joust is grounded in intricate awareness and understanding of the importance of authority as personhood. For tens of generations, people in the region were subjected to highly unequal and brutal forms of social organisation. Under medieval feudalism, the vast majority of people within a society were peasants whose lives as 'serfs' were heavily controlled by their landlords and lords. They were born into that status and died in that status. Their position was justified by the notion that they had been conquered or subjugated and therefore were dependent upon their superiors for their subsistence. This placed people in a position of perpetual indebtedness. In effect, people were only recognised as 'persons' with actual agency if they owned their own land and had the ability to sustain themselves independently. This meant that people were subject to appalling exploitation and abuse. While the legal basis of serfdom reduced over time, it persisted in relationships like 'the hinds',[18] who were farm labourers tied in general service to landlords for fixed terms and 'the bond'[19] that tied miners to an exclusive period of labour to specific mine owners.

Dependence created very real and very bad consequences for people. These would become ever more real, and worse, as dependence deepened through debt. As such, people sought as fully as possible to avoid indebtedness, controlling spending, maintaining budgets and saving where possible.[20] The historian Sean O'Connell charts this through the lives of various working-class people in the 19th and 20th centuries:

> John Moores was born in Eccles in 1896. … John's father was a bricklayer who, at one point, also part-owned a public house. However, this financial interest developed into a taste for the pub's chief product and alcoholism and violence made the marriage an unhappy one. … Young John watched his mother secretly pawn her husband's gold watch to help with family finances. Eventually, debts forced her business to collapse and Louisa was compelled to take in washing to make ends meet, visibly tumbling down the social hierarchy in the process. … John's early life experience had provided a stark lesson in the hazards that faced the working-class family and of the difficulties of retaining respectable status in a world filled with economic uncertainties and judgemental onlookers. His mother's experience of debt, and the loss of personal autonomy that it brought her, left a deep imprint. Until his death, in 1993, he constantly urged his family to take a cautious approach to consumer credit.[21]

Awareness of the relationship between receiving goods, debt and autonomy is one of the key reasons that the discourse of austerity, and of the Big Society, found favour, among older people in particular.[22] Belt tightening is a long-standing response to having low incomes in a deeply unequal society. It is responsible insofar as it upholds people's authority as individuals by preventing others from exploiting our weakness. Indeed, this is one of the key reasons why working-class communities supported mutual aid, building societies, credit unions and trade unionism – all institutions that enhanced financial security without exposing people to domination by those who owned land and industry. The creation of the welfare state after the Second World War was the natural next step to this: an impersonal provision of financial security that protected us from indebtedness to, and domination by, those with more resources than us.

Yet, many of us who have not experienced long-term, secure employment now see no means of avoiding personal debt. Indeed, many of our lives revolve around it. Whether through hire purchases, 'pay day' loans, rent arrears and any number of other debts to any number of creditors, many of us often place ourselves in positions of subjugation to satisfy our basic needs.[23] The consequence has been dramatic. Often, our home and its contents belong wholly to others. Many of us are accustomed to those with authority, such as bailiffs and Local Authority officers, wandering into our houses and asserting authority over the contents. Stripped of authority, people have no power left to exercise save to choose whether to open the door or watch it being kicked in. As a female resident of Ashington put it, many of us are used to circumstances in which vulnerability leads to homes being taken away and children being separated from parents and siblings and traumatised.[24]

It is the loss of support and security from the government, not its receipt, that has reduced people to positions of passivity and hopelessness.[25] The long-term process of neoliberal reform has dissolved the social bonds and institutions that protected us from domination in the past.[26] The loss of basic rites, like tea and biscuits, reflects a loss of authority and being resigned to our fate. In order to function as social actors, we need authority to act, and that authority is fundamentally associated with entitlement: the entitlement to our resources and to the spheres within which we act. Such entitlement can only come from knowing that our basic resources are fundamentally ours and can't be taken away by specific individuals. This is why basic income, as a statutory entitlement, is potentially transformative, first for individuals and their sense of self, and through them to relationships and hence communities.

## The inefficiency of the current system, revisited

It is worth exploring, once more, the chaos that our current economic model produces. In our study of Northeast GPs,[27] the doctors described a set of circumstances in which services were being overwhelmed by the weight of avoidable ill health. They described their role in sustaining the benefits system, viewing consultations as means of legitimising welfare claims (or not). One recalled a case in which a patient in receipt of disability benefit sought to continue treatment of pain through opiates, despite their ineffectiveness and side effects, since '"Requiring morphine" was seen as a marker of severity, even though the morphine was ineffective.' Another stated that 'You want to prove to the state that you're as ill, and disabled, and incapable as you possibly can otherwise your kids might starve.' Life within our current benefits system was described as 'almost like a full-time job', with one GP stating that they had gradually shifted away from encouraging work because of the negative consequences of inactivity and worklessness, and towards an almost unquestioning provision of support for claims in order that those who have genuine need are not deprived of essential resources.

For those in paid work, the situation was just as bad, marked by 'stress from bad working practices' and 'feeling bullied by employers'. The constraints imposed by increasingly precarious employment contracts affected the ability of patients to attend medical appointments. In consequence, while many people receiving welfare support had a disincentive to get well, many of those in paid work had a disincentive to seek treatment. Those in precarious employment '[were] more likely to work through periods of sickness, even if it would aid their recovery to have time off. This can mean that periods of illness are lengthened or have longer-term consequences. E.g. manual labourers who choose to work through episodes of mechanical back pain'.

These are lived experiences of a dysfunctional system that makes us unwell. By making poverty, inequality and insecurity worse upstream, our current institutions create insurmountable pressure on services downstream. GPs become agents of the welfare system, police officers become social workers, and those of us in need of welfare become stuck on administrative treadmills in pursuit of support that turns out to be inadequate.

Against this backdrop, the GPs reached many of the conclusions about basic income that we have discussed in this book: that basic income 'would be a solution for all the pointless sick note system, the pointless reports to the benefits agency'; would eliminate the 'shame', stigma and 'humiliating' process of form-filling to prove individual need. It would support 'people who are currently not rewarded – informal carers, housewives, people bringing up kids'.

### Forward to the past, or forward to the future?

As well as the positive consequences of introducing basic income, it is worth considering the negative consequences of failing to do so. We know what a future without basic income looks like: it looks like the past. This was the past in which our ancestors were forced to take bad risks, and denied the ability to take good ones.[28]

In 1927, long before the welfare reforms that rebuilt Britain in 1945, Peter McCartney, the great-great-great-grandfather of two members of our author group, was working as a joiner at Armstrong, Whitworth & Co. in Walker, Tyneside. At the end of his shift, he had to work on staging, which the stagers had recognised was insecure. Carpenters were called, but were busy. Because Peter was paid by price – a set price for the work completed – he had good reason not to wait. The delay would cause him to lose other work.

Given how low his pay was, losing the work would prevent his feeding his family. So, he climbed the staging, and it collapsed. He was wounded and the wound turned septic. Because of the absence of decent healthcare in the days before the National Health Service, he died. He was 69 years old and left behind a destitute wife and disabled family members. Had he had a basic income to fall back on, he would have had the authority to refuse any demand to climb staging that he knew was unsafe. That was a bad risk to take, but he took it because he couldn't afford not to. There are men and women across our country who are now taking bad – often fatal – risks that they would not have taken until recently and would not take were they socially secure. The statutory entitlement to basic income gives people the authority to say no.

In 1956, Tommy Johnson, the grandfather of the same authors, was a gas fitter for the Gas Board. He was a talented and capable technician who worked on his family's houses well into his 70s. His foreman recognised his talent and offered him a unique opportunity. If he resigned from his job, he would be offered a monopoly on cooker repairs at the Gas Board yard. He would go from being employed to self-employed – his own man. This self-employment would offer a higher income and potential for expansion. If he performed well, there would be an opportunity to take on repairs at other yards across the region. It was the opportunity to create a business that would give work, not just to him, but eventually to his son and other relatives.

But coming from a family with no wealth and with two growing kids, he decided that he would need several times the £20 he had saved to his name just to tide him over between his final pay cheque and his first invoice. In the absence of familial wealth, the only means of covering the bridging period would be by taking out loans with high rates of interest. Doing that would place him and his family in a position of being dominated by individuals with more wealth. As such, he returned to his foreman the next day and said that he couldn't take the risk. Which responsible parent could take the risk of not being able to feed their family?

For the rest of his life, he cursed what he saw as foolishness. He spent his last two decades fighting industrial-related diseases on a council estate that went from bad to worse by the day – dominated by those around him and their antisocial behaviour. The cooker repair opportunity was a good risk to take, but he couldn't afford to take it because he had nothing to fall back on. He had no authority to act, because he had no entitlement to social security.

These are cases from history, but these things are still happening now. They happen every day, to so many hardworking people.

Now, more than ever, tradespeople are subcontracted for price work – work that depends on completion of single tasks. They take risks they shouldn't: roofers with stomas from previous falls climbing steep pitched roofs dosed up with opiates; builders handling asbestos because they know that removing it properly would take time they can't afford to take. They perform less well than they know they can because they have to work as quickly as possible, even if it means cutting corners. Concern over the standard of new-build housing is driven by this. But the biggest problem is that people in so many professions are flogging themselves into the ground, because they feel they have to. They are knackered and they often can't see any possibility of things improving.

For younger workers, it is getting harder and harder to do what Tommy Johnson wished he'd done and make things better for their families. It's just not possible to train, build businesses and take good risks, even when taking those risks benefits everyone. Our younger people are stuck, and their children will be even more stuck, just like generations of peasants from the past. This costs us all: the loss of social dynamism, and the cost of addressing the health consequences downstream.

The irony is that, in our country, there are people with basic income. They're the rich, the privileged, people with wealth from their parents. Some are the descendants of the likes of Armstrong & Whitworth, of people who profited from Peter McCartney's decades of labour and poverty. They benefit from our workers being returned to the powerlessness of the past. They know that they will never have to take harmful risks, and can quite happily take good risks, because they have their families' wealth to fall back on. Their children are likely to benefit even more greatly from the concentration of wealth and opportunity.

This situation is not just unfair: it's bad for our economy and society. It means that talented people are denied the opportunities that they have earned. It is impossible to calculate the cost to Britain of this stifling of contribution. Only basic income gives us the ability to feel the benefit of the good ideas and talented people we can develop in our communities if we enable people to take good risks.

## Case Study: The double dividend in action among tradespeople in Darlington

The need among tradespeople for financial security has been central to changing minds on basic income. Journalist Anoosh Chakalian has described this in an interview with Graeme Feeney, 46, a builder from Darlington who attended the Jarrow launch of plans for basic income pilots in the town. He thought 'it would open up a can of worms – I know people who have problems spending too much on drinking, drugs or gambling'. However, Chakalian notes that:

> [A]s a self-employed tradesman, Feeney reflected that a system like this would have helped him take time out to heal after he sliced two fingers off while working in 2002 (instead, in need of wages, he returned to work days after his surgery, his wound became infected and he now has limited use of his hand). He's also noticed colleagues struggle. He knows one 68-year-old joiner who can't afford to retire, and another 19-year-old in the same trade who couldn't afford university. 'I've seen it from both ends of the spectrum: people should have so much more opportunity in life.'[29]

Across the country, those of us who make our infrastructure, who build our houses, who run their bodies into the ground in enabling us to live, can only do well in today's climate through the security that basic income provides. For too long, the absence of welfare support for tradespeople has been used to drum up opposition to welfare payments to those of us who are out of employment or unable to do paid work. Basic income is fundamental to enabling us to rebuild Britain.

7

# If you like basic income, you're in the majority

In the previous chapters, we argued that basic income is a highly beneficial reform, in a panoply of intertwined ways. This begs the question: if this is such a great policy, why has it not been implemented anywhere in the world? Closer at hand, why do neither of the two main UK political parties advocate its introduction? The second question is related to the first: for a reform to be implemented in a democracy generally takes one or all of the main political parties to make it their business. A supportive party must be in power to enact the relevant legislation. Also, political parties play an important role in orchestrating political conversation, and hence creating social momentum around a reform. Basic income will only happen if major parties make it their business.

For the Conservative Party, the answer to the second question is perhaps relatively easy. That party primarily represents the interests of those who wish to see the welfare state retrenched and made cheaper, rather than made better. For decades, they have been committed to a model in which the state does less than it currently does. Many of them would like to see it largely wither away, leaving people to use the private sector to seek the services they need. We said the argument was *relatively* easy, because even if this is your aim, basic income has attractive features. Figures like Milton Friedman and Friedrich Hayek are generally seen as belonging to the small-state, pro-market tradition, and they favoured government-provided minimum incomes. There are certainly good reasons for liking basic income if you like your state lean, efficient and non-interfering. Nonetheless, the present

Conservative Party finds raising taxation unpalatable, even if the payoffs and savings are very large. (Here, we are talking about the party. As we shall see later in the chapter, people who vote for the party are more open to tax rises than you might imagine, as long as the effects are sufficiently good.) All in all, the lack of enthusiasm for basic income coming from the Conservative Party is not too great a puzzle.

A greater mystery lies in the Labour Party. The Labour Party represents a movement historically committed to improving the lives of working people. This is what basic income would do, very efficiently and directly, for the great bulk of the population. One would imagine that Labour would vociferously have supported the policy when in opposition, and paved the way for it when in government. This goes for centre-left parties in other affluent countries too. A major answer to the puzzle of non-existence of basic income institutions in the world so far is that the mainstream centre-left in Europe and the Americas has not made the introduction of such institutions its business.

We think that this is the direction mainstream centre-left parties should move in if they wish to remain relevant. But it is worth dwelling a little on why their enthusiasm for basic income has so far been so underwhelming.

One part is historical. Centre-left movements were born out of the desire to improve the lives of ordinary people, particularly those that must work just to get to the end of the month. The solution those movements initially identified was through better *collective* bargaining organised through *workplaces* (think, for example, of how a trades union functions and gains its power). This was later supported by centre-left governments running industrial strategies that kept those workplaces going. This made a lot of sense in the context of the period: most people worked in large workplaces where they had potentially long tenure; the salaries from those single workplaces were sufficient to keep households afloat, or could be bargained to a high enough level to do so. But basic income represents a very different kind of solution. It provides *individual* bargaining power *independently of* any particular workplace. It provides a kind of autonomy at the individual level that comes from people knowing that they will never be in dire straits, whether they choose to stay in their current job (and union) or not. This is a philosophically rather different way of helping working people. We have argued it is a more appropriate one for the phase of economic development that we live in, with the inadequacy of wages, the rise of self-employment, the shift to services, the gig economy and the precariat. To some extent, centre-left movements just have not caught up yet. At times, indeed, they have viewed this alternative way of enacting their historic mission with some suspicion, so different is it from their habitual way of thinking.

There is another important element to the reluctance of political parties, including those of the centre-left, to campaign for basic income. They often hold, rather oddly, the idea that it would not be popular. For example, in 2023, the centre-left newspaper *The Guardian* ran a review of a book called *Free and Equal*, by Daniel Chandler.[1] Chandler's book presents a good argument for the introduction of basic income, funded by higher taxation, from a left-liberal perspective. Nice arguments, the review implies, but it would be electoral suicide to go and try and sell *that* to the Red Wall. The Red Wall describes a swathe of parliamentary seats in the Midlands and North of England with large working-class populations. The implication of the review was that most people in Red Wall populations are socially conservative, and unwilling to countenance bold proposals for progressive reform. (This is despite those populations containing many people in poverty, and usually being represented by Labour MPs, as they overwhelmingly are at present.) To win power, you need to win over the Red Wall. Presenting a proposal like basic income would be a short route to political irrelevance, as even the potential beneficiaries in the Red Wall would find it viscerally unacceptable. So obvious was this fact to *The Guardian*'s reviewer that he did not feel obliged to provide any evidence for it.

This seemed odd to us. We have been carrying out research on public opinion relating to basic income for years, some of it the UK population in general, and some specifically in Red Wall constituencies. What we find is not at all what *The Guardian* reviewer assumed; not in the Red Wall, and not in the rest of the country either. As we will outline in this chapter, we have found: broad consensus that the status quo is not working; an extremely high level of support for redistributive reforms; very high support for basic income in particular; and a very broad willingness to see taxes raised if the payoffs for doing so were big enough. The picture is nuanced. Many people, especially the young, love the idea of basic income and find it an obvious solution. A small minority of people strongly dislikes basic income at first sight. Engaging with these individuals reveals that they often like it much better at second sight, that is to say, after thinking through the arguments in its favour. Finding the best arguments for basic income was something we let the most entrenched Red Wall opponents do for us; they were very good at it, as we shall see in what follows.

Another important reason that people are apathetic or unenthusiastic about basic income proposals is not that they think they are a bad idea; it's that they think politicians are so inept at implementing good ideas that it's not worth bothering to try. People in this state of mind include many of those most sick and disadvantaged by the current status quo. They – a potentially important constituency driving for change – don't push for reforms that would be to their advantage, because they think those reforms would get corrupted or botched in the implementation, leaving the populace no better off, and perhaps worse. This is an important challenge for basic income advocates, or for those favouring any kind of progressive reform: getting the populace to trust that they could deliver. We think basic income could be part of the solution here.[2] It is a simple, central reform that centre-left parties could champion; that, under scheme 1, could be put in place quickly; and that would have immediate and widespread effects on many people's lives. Basic income could do for the current Labour government what taking the doctor's bill out of people's hands did between 1945 and 1951: provide an everyday, homely, reminder of why progressive politics is worth supporting, and worth believing in.

The rest of this chapter reviews the evidence around the popularity of basic income, and the conundrum that this popular policy is viewed by many politicians as electorally unpalatable. What is the truth? Would enough people vote for it yet? And, if not, how can we bring about the social conversation leading to that point?

## What does the polling evidence say?

Basic income has become a sufficiently serious part of the political conversation as to get investigated through opinion polling. A 2016 survey presented basic income, with a detailed description and a single 'Strongly in favour/In favour/Against/Strongly against' question, to representative samples from 23 European countries including the UK. The proportions strongly in favour or in favour exceeded 45 per cent in 20 of the 23 countries, only Sweden, Norway and Switzerland recording lower proportions.[3] The proportion in favour or strongly so in the UK in this survey was slightly over 50 per cent. Across the countries, support was rather stronger among participants who were younger, doing less well financially, and had more left-wing orientations or goals.

As the Dutch researchers who wrote up the study put it, with enjoyable understatement, 'support for basic income seems to be rather overwhelming'. However, while 45 per cent or 50 per cent of votes would easily win a general election, it is not yet the groundswell of public opinion that makes an outcome politically inevitable soon. Recent support for nationalisation of railways and water services in the UK is closer to 70 per cent.[4] This is a level at which even the Labour Party feels emboldened to act. Once public support is around 70 per cent or so, it is not just that a mainstream political party can make the issue its business; it is that it cannot *not* do so, and survive.

We have carried out more detailed research on support for basic income in the UK, both nationally and in respondents from Red Wall constituencies. Our findings echo the general patterns from the 2016 international survey, with the crucial difference that the absolute levels of support are consistently higher. They are closer to the 70 per cent benchmark than the 50 per cent. It is difficult to say whether this is due to differences in our methods, or a rapid increase in support for basic income. We suspect the latter. Part of this may be due to the general increase over time in the ills that basic income addresses, and in part to greater public discussion of basic income and basic income trials in the last few years. Another part may have been specifically caused by the COVID-19 pandemic. In the pandemic, people saw with their own eyes how the need for financial support can fluctuate unpredictably and very rapidly, drawing in all kinds of people who never dreamed they would require state aid. They saw that a retrospective conditional system could not keep up. They also saw how a bold, broad, prospective intervention by the state, in the form of the COVID-19-era Job Retention Scheme, popularly known as 'furlough', could have a welcome transformative effect.

In the summer of 2021, we surveyed 850 respondents from 42 Red Wall constituencies in England.[5] In our academic articles, we applied weightings to the responses, to make our sample more representative of the English electorate, but here we present the unweighted numbers to give you a sense of what the raw mood looked like. (Weighting makes very little difference, in fact.) A difference from the 2016 international survey is that we asked everyone to give their *degree* of support on a continuous, 0–100 scale, so 0 is total opposition and 100 is the strongest support imaginable.

The arithmetic mean support level was 76; the median was 81. Two hundred and thirty-two people gave the maximum possible rating of 100; 477 a rating of 80 or more; and 749, a rating of 50 or more. In other words, only 99 people, or around 11 per cent, rated their support below the neutral point of 50/100. We will come back to this opposed group later. Breaking down the sample revealed broadly the same patterns as in the international survey (Figure 7.1). Younger people supported basic income more strongly than older people. Homeownership, which we use here as a rough proxy for economic security, was associated with lower support compared to non-ownership. Having voted for the Labour Party at the 2019 general election, as a proxy for being somewhat left-wing in orientation, was associated with higher support than having voted for the Conservative Party, with other parties in between.

These subgroup variations, however, can distract us from an important message in these data. Support was *surprisingly high in the groups among whom support is the lowest*. The median support among 50–64-year-olds, the age group with the lowest support, was still 79, against 84 for the 18–34s. The median for homeowners was still 80, against 88 for non-owners. The median for people who voted Conservative at the 2019 general election was (astonishingly) 70 of a possible 100, against 88 for

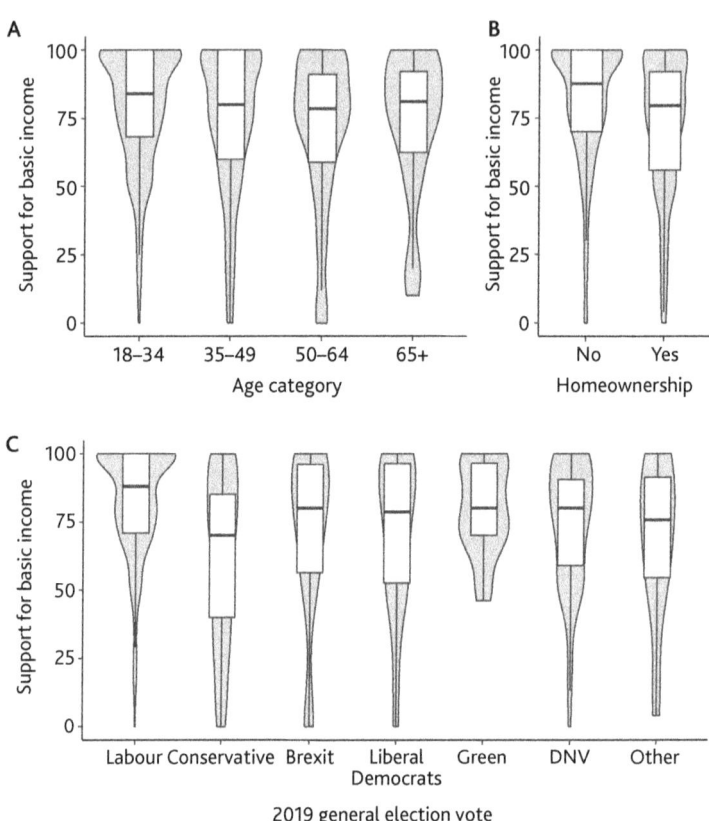

**Figure 7.1:** Distribution of support for basic income, on a 0–100 scale, in the Red Wall survey, broken down by age group (A), homeownership (B) and 2019 general election vote (C)

Notes: The dark band represents the median, and the box represents the range from the 25th percentile of responses to the 75th percentile. DNV = did not vote.

Source: Adapted from M. Johnson, E. Johnson and D. Nettle, 'Are "Red Wall" Constituencies Really Opposed to Progressive Policy? Examining the Impact of Materialist Narratives for Universal Basic Income', *British Politics* 18 (2022): 104–127.

those who voted Labour. These findings, then, suggest not just very strong support for the policy among the young, left-wing precariat of the Red Wall, but also the possibility of assembling a very broad supportive coalition. This survey was at the tail end of the COVID-19 pandemic era, and this may have boosted support. However, we have no evidence that levels of support would be lower now.

A possible caveat with these findings is that the survey did not differentiate between introducing basic income, and doing *anything at all* to reduce poverty and inequality. We might have been picking up the consensus that people should be getting more help, rather than a preference for basic income over possible alternative forms of help. It is possible that if we had presented the question in the format 'Which would you rather the government did, introduce basic income, or make the existing benefits system more generous?', people would have opted for the latter in large numbers. We have one dataset that did ask this, from a year earlier, at the height of the COVID-19 pandemic. This sample was UK-wide rather specific to the Red Wall. Here we found the majority of people preferring a basic income system to a conditional one that we deliberately described as being equally generous, both in the context of the then-current pandemic, and for hypothetical 'normal times' in which the pandemic had not happened.[6] The level of preference for basic income over the conditional alternative was not as striking as the high level of support for basic income when presented in the absence of any alternative reform, though. This suggests that the high support for basic income that we observe in surveys of the UK is partly about people genuinely liking the design features of the policy, and partly the general hunger for something – anything – to be done about poverty and inequality in the UK.

## What happens when we talk about the price tag?

When *The Guardian* reviewer assumed that basic income was unsaleable in the Red Wall, he was probably not thinking that people were opposed to the basic income coming in as such. Rather, he was assuming that few people in the Red Wall are ready to vote for the tax rises likely to be needed to fund it. It is certainly true that when you make the costs of the scheme salient, you elicit lower levels of support than when you do not mention them. Some people have taken this to imply that support for basic income is not really high enough to make the reform electorally credible. Basic income is only appealing in a daydream, fantasy way.

Our answer is: of course support goes down when you emphasise the costs. It would be weird if it did not. If I ask you how much you would like to go out for a delicious meal, and then how much you would like to go out for a delicious meal that costs rather a lot, obviously I will elicit less enthusiasm and more caution in the second case. If there were a delicious meal out available that cost nothing, you would eat it. But, knowing this does not mean you would never go out for a delicious meal that costs rather a lot, given that delicious meals out are not available for free in practice. What we need to understand is how your motivation to consume a meal out is affected by both its deliciousness in one direction, and its cost in the other. In other words, what we need to do is understand how voters would *trade off* the benefits of basic income against the costs to them in personal taxation.

One way of doing this is via a conjoint survey. In a conjoint survey, we generate many hypothetical policies with different combinations of features: policies that increase poverty, reduce poverty by 10 per cent, by 20 per cent, don't change poverty; policies that decrease income tax by three pence in the pound, don't change it, or increase it. We then ask people to choose repeatedly the policy they prefer from a pair, a little like the optician who puts two different lenses in front of your eye: better with *this* one, or with *this* one? By looking in detail at which policies are chosen more often, we can infer the trade-off function that drives people's decisions.

We carried out a conjoint survey for basic income schemes of different generosities in the UK in 2022.[7] Our proposed policies varied from one another on several dimensions, but we will simplify the results here. The main thing we identified was a simple trade-off axis. On the one hand, the more a reform reduced poverty, the more respondents liked it, other things being equal. On the other hand, the higher the rates of personal income tax the reform required, the less they liked it, other things being equal. This means that if there were a policy that reduced poverty but did not involve raising personal taxation, almost everyone would choose it; and if there were a policy to cut personal taxation that did not involve increasing poverty (or having any other negative effects not covered within our survey),

## If you like basic income, you're in the majority

most people would choose that. The critical question is: when a policy *both* reduces poverty, and increases personal taxation, which consideration wins out?

In this sample, the poverty-reduction motivation often won out. We can visualise this by plotting policies on the two axes of their effect on poverty, and their required personal income tax rates (Figure 7.2). On Figure 7.2, pale grey indicates that a policy with that combination was generally preferred to the status quo, and dark grey that it was generally dispreferred. The status quo itself is shown with cross-hatching. We have plotted the results separately for respondents who voted for the Conservative Party, and the Labour Party, in 2019. People who voted for any other party, or did not vote at all, were somewhere in between. We have also run the results separately by other groupings, such as men and women or young and old, and the basic findings are always much the same.

On both plots, we can see that there is a zone of possible electoral advantage for basic income schemes that both increase personal taxation and reduce poverty. There is a kind of

**Figure 7.2:** Visualisation of trade-off between personal income tax rates and poverty, separated by Labour (left) and Conservative (right) voting in 2019

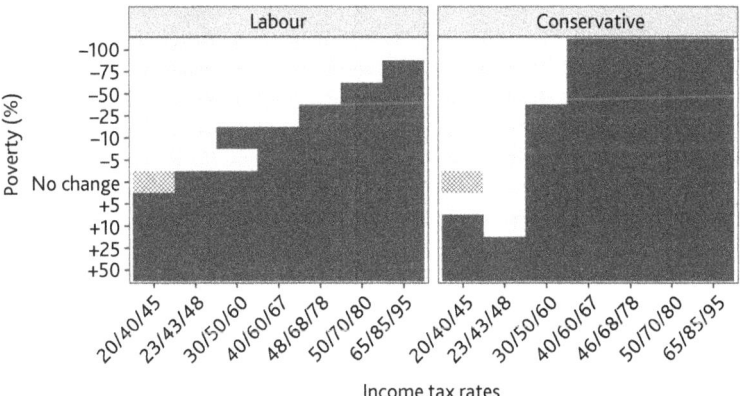

Notes: The dark shading shows a combination of income tax rates and poverty that would be dispreferred to the status quo, other things being equal, and pale shading shows combinations that would be preferred to the status quo. The status quo is shown cross-hatched.

Source: Adapted from D. Nettle, J. Chrisp, E.A. Johnson and M.T. Johnson, 'What Do People Want from a Welfare System? Conjoint Survey Evidence from UK Adults', Working Paper, 21 September 2023, https://doi.org/10.31235/osf.io/zfnuh.

proportionality here: the higher the required tax rates, the better the effect on poverty has to be in order to justify the intervention. But, critically, voters from both Labour and Conservative groups had a pale grey zone where personal taxation was substantially higher than it is at present, and still the policy was preferred to the status quo. As one would predict, the zones had slightly different shapes for the two groups, with Labour voters tolerating higher taxes to obtain a given level of poverty reduction, and Conservative voters unwilling to go beyond a certain level of taxation however large the poverty benefits. But the more striking generalisation is that *both* groups have a zone where they are willing to pay more for an effective reform that reduces poverty. They only disagree about its boundaries. There are thus plenty of possible reforms that are pale grey for everyone. This means, again, that it should be possible to design a redistributive, anti-poverty programme whose support is not very partisan. It could command support from coalitions of young and old; rich and poor; left, centre and right.

This study also found that funding basic income policies through wealth tax, tax on corporate profits or corporate carbon taxes made them especially popular. The way we can think of this is that such moves square the circle of reducing poverty and inequality without increasing deductions from individuals so much. Given that so much of the economic growth of the last 30 years has been captured by capital, not labour, and given the need to make the economy more sustainable because of the climate crisis, we think these approaches to raising revenue for the more ambitious basic income policies like our schemes 2 and 3 make a great deal of sense, both electorally and economically.

### Why do people like (and dislike) basic income?

There is some variation in how much people like the idea of basic income. Perhaps we can exploit this variation to understand why support for the policy in the UK seems to be growing. In our 2021 study, we asked how important various considerations were to them in the design of a welfare system, and also how much they supported basic income.[8] They liked basic income more when: they thought simplicity of administration was more important; they thought stress and anxiety reduction was a more important goal; and they assigned more priority to valuing every individual. All three factors – simplicity of administration, need to reduce stress and need to value everyone – had become more important in people's minds during the COVID-19 pandemic. We suspect these considerations are becoming more important over time in general, pandemic aside, with the rise of precarity and inequality, and the cost of living crisis. The shifting balance of priorities may be driving the obvious increase in public discussion of basic income.

One factor that negatively predicted support for basic income is worth singling out. The more worried respondents were about 'undeserving' people getting support, the less they liked basic income. This fits with an established academic literature on the 'deservingness' heuristic:[9] the assumption that to get a benefit from society, you have to deserve it. Deservingness can come from having paid your dues at other times; or at least trying hard, or your need being genuine and not your fault. It is to cater to a perceived deservingness heuristic in the voting public (rather than any actual practical effectiveness) that politicians are fond of trumpeting workfare-style conditionality, and making medical assessments ever-stricter.[10]

Although our 2021 data confirmed that respondents were somewhat concerned about deservingness, and that deservingness motivations generally gave them reservations about basic income, this was a weaker influence than we expected. It was statistically swamped in this study by the desirability of a simple system that valued everyone and reduced stress. The perceived importance of deservingness considerations may have waned over time, as people have witnessed the social expansion of insecurity and want. We return to the deservingness issue in what follows, as, in one way or another, it plays a rather central role in argumentative challenges to basic income, and hence the reluctance of some politicians to commit to the reform.

### Argumentative justifications

People support reforms if they can understand those reforms as being in their interests. We take a broad view of what 'interests' can include. It is a great deal more encompassing than just the individual monetary bottom line, though that does play a role. History is full of examples of people voting for things that are not to their immediate, narrow financial advantage. 'Interests', as we understand them, incorporate returns not only in the currency of money, but more importantly in the currency of capability: what kinds of lives will the reform give me the capability to have, if I so choose? They also incorporate returns beyond the self: to family, to friends, to neighbours and fellow citizens. Thus, 'interests' can drive a desire not just for individual wealth, but also security, access to important services when needed, and more intangible societal benefits, like living in a community that is functional, not full of rancour or indignity, and in which there is a liveable public space.

However, 'interests', even defined as broadly as we do here, are not the only determinant of willingness to advocate for a reform. Humans, uniquely as far as we are aware, also want to be able to give a reasonable account of their preferences to their peers.[11] It's very uncomfortable to support an action – whatever the pragmatic payoffs – unless one can look others in the eye and make a reasonable case that the action is a good one. Thus, there are two tests that a proposed reform must meet in order to become implementable. Enough people must come to believe that the reform is in their interests; and enough people must be able to think of argumentative justifications for the reform that they find good enough for conversation.

A major block to the development of basic income schemes has been in the sphere of argumentative justifications. There is a situation that every politician dreads: finding themselves on the doorstep campaigning, or in an interview with a hostile journalist, being faced with the question 'Why should I give my money to people who have done nothing in return?', having nothing very clear to say, floundering and looking idiotic. This is why politicians are ultra-safe in the reforms they will support; why they hedge rather than avoiding questions; and why, often, they would rather retreat into strategic ambiguity than defend a concrete policy. The problem of argumentative justification does not uniquely afflict professional politicians; it arises for anyone who is going to discuss basic income in a workplace or political meeting.

Needless to say, we think there are good argumentative justifications for basic income: you just have to think about it in the right way. We have outlined some of those justifications in this book, and elsewhere.[12] The philosophical literature on basic income is centrally devoted to this problem.[13] In our empirical work on the popularity of basic income, we were less concerned with the argumentative justifications that *we* could come up with, and more concerned with which justifications voters might articulate and find acceptable.

To study this problem, we decided to focus on respondents who, in our Red Wall survey, were strongly opposed to the introduction of basic income. As we mentioned earlier, this was a small minority; but it only takes a small, devoted minority to raise uncomfortable problems of argumentative justification.

We recontacted 20 people who had been opposed or strongly opposed to the policy. We noted their opposition, but asked them nonetheless to spend 15 minutes coming up with an argument that they thought might convince their friends and families that basic income was a good idea. They were working online and may have consulted the internet; we don't know how much they relied on this.

The 20 narratives they produced varied in length and style, but we could spot some recurring arguments. We were thus able to condense them into six pro-basic income narratives of 160–180 words. At the risk of trying the reader's patience, we reproduce all six in full here. Though the editing is ours, the thrust of the arguments, the examples and much of the exact wording comes from the respondents. (Note: in this study, we referred to basic income as Universal Basic Income [UBI]. Nothing important turns on this shift in terminology.)

> **Narrative one:** This country is in a terrible mess at the moment. Health aside, the COVID-19 situation has caused untold misery, stress and economic uncertainty to millions of people. The economy is on its knees as businesses fold and jobs are lost hand over fist across the private sector. Families are struggling, rent and mortgage payments are being missed. People do not have as much disposable income to spend in local

businesses, meaning entire communities are dying. By giving us all regular, predictable, secure income, UBI would give the economy a vital boost, kick-starting growth and bringing back confidence to businesses and consumers alike. It would also help create a smaller, simpler state as civil servants are moved from the large Department of Work and Pensions to deal with other more pressing issues, such as health. A smaller state could lead to reduction in the overall rate of taxation, helping boost stock markets and new industries. UBI is the simple answer to bring our society back from the brink of total disaster.

**Narrative two:** By paying all of us regularly, regardless of whether we work or not, UBI is a social contract for all of society. As such, we need evidence that there are obvious benefits for society as a whole. Evidence currently shows that it does not reduce willingness to work and increases health and entrepreneurship throughout society. The best evidence in support of introducing UBI can be seen in the COVID-19 furlough payments and the temporary rise in Universal Credit. Although there was some inflation, there was no hyperinflation and the government itself declared that there was no effect on willingness to work. Before UBI is gradually introduced, the criteria for evaluating the policy will be laid down and its impacts will be monitored by the Office for National Statistics. The policy will be tailored according to those established impacts and there will be continuous assessments of affordability to ensure there is a net benefit over the economic cycle.

**Narrative three:** UBI gives you the financial security that the wealthy and those on long-term benefits take for granted. With a regular, unconditional payment, you would be able to educate yourself and develop your business ideas, making you and your family better off in the process. This is just levelling the playing field for talented, hard-working people who strive to get ahead, but can't take the risk of taking time out. As someone who gets up and goes to work every day, you currently get nothing back from the government. Unlike both Universal Credit and the furlough scheme, UBI does not discriminate against you. You will not be paying taxes with no reward. This is peace of mind for working people. If you are self-employed, this is a buffer for times when you are ill or on holiday. If you are employed, why not see this money as a nice bonus? However you use it, take it, enjoy it and be grateful that, for once, we're getting money back for a change!

**Narrative four:** The current welfare system disincentives work for several reasons. It has an extremely high marginal 'tax' rate, which means that the benefit is withdrawn too quickly as income increases. It then takes too long to be reinstated when income reduces. In order to receive disability-related benefits, you have to demonstrate that you are completely inactive. Making yourself healthier by being active, socialising and participating in society increases the chances of losing benefits. Having disincentives to work traps people in poverty, not just economically, but psychologically too. Being unable to provide for yourself is debilitating. It is bad for self-respect and mental health and provides a bad example for children. Counter-intuitively, evidence suggests that, where UBI is introduced, these disincentives to work are removed. This is because, by paying all of us regularly, there are no longer disincentives stopping you from working and you are no longer stigmatised for receiving benefits. This means that you have the ability to be active, better yourself and provide the best role model for your children.

**Narrative five:** The UK welfare system is long overdue for reform. Universal Credit was supposed to replace previous complicated schemes, but has been extremely inefficient. Claiming it requires you to fill in various complicated forms. It takes weeks to receive the first payment and is withdrawn too quickly when people start to earn small amounts of money. This means they stop your benefits when you need them again quite quickly. That puts your entire life on hold, leaving you to rely on high interest payday lenders like Wonga for cashflow. UBI guarantees everyone weekly income when you don't earn without fear of it being cancelled when you do. Paying everyone regardless of work status, age and amount of savings may at first seem extravagant and wasteful. However, the cost of administering means tested schemes far exceeds any payments to those who would be ineligible at present. In 2020/2021, there was an estimated loss to the nation of £7.6 billion from fraud or error. UBI eradicates this and leads to a slimmer, simpler state for us all to navigate.

**Narrative six:** UBI is a living pension for all adult citizens, providing state support for your basic needs. It would be a safety net during short periods of unemployment, giving you some time to support yourself and your family while looking for employment. This helps to stop you slipping into poverty and ensures that you do not face homelessness. As many infamous cases have shown, this is vital for us, as the current system does not keep us secure. There was the case of the diabetic British War Veteran whose Universal Credit payment lapsed, leaving him with no money to top up his electricity meter. This meant that he could not keep his medicine refrigerated, meaning that he went into a diabetic coma and died. In our country, you should not have the stress of worrying about meeting your basic needs. You should not have to worry that taking on short-term work will leave you unable to support yourself. UBI secures you from the many unpredictable events in modern society.

These texts present a canny combination of concrete examples and broad justificatory principles. They stress that basic income is a policy for all of us, not just an 'othered' subgroup of the unemployed or indigent. It is heartening to see that many of the arguments that have interested us, as academics, were prominent. The ability of the participants – self-professed opponents of basic income – to generate compelling argumentative justifications shows that justification is to some extent the work of the imagination. It is informed by the facts and experiences that are lying around, but it goes beyond these and put them together, for the purposes of communicative expression, in transformative ways.

In the next step, we conducted a new survey, also in broadly Red Wall constituencies, this time including some constituencies in Wales. We identified a further group of respondents strongly opposed to basic income. We then had each of these opponents (105 respondents in total) read one of the six narratives and say how much they supported basic income *after* reading it.

Participants changed their views on basic income, quite strikingly. They went from supporting basic income at around 15 on the 100-point scale on average (remember, the participants were chosen because of how opposed they were), to around 47. The experiment lacks a control condition, unfortunately. This would be a condition where a group of participants are asked for their support for basic income a second time without reading a justification narrative in the interim. Perhaps just thinking about it a second time increases support. We suspect that the narratives are doing a big part of the job. People reported that their views had been affected by what they read, and the size of their uplift in support for basic income was related to how much they said the narrative had affected them.

There was minor variation in how persuasive people found the narratives (narrative six being judged the most persuasive, and narrative two the least), but all six were all rated at least moderately persuasive. There was also some evidence of differential impact according to the age of the reader. Young people were differentially persuaded by narrative six, and to a lesser extent narrative three. These narratives stress the provision of personal economic security ('peace of mind for working people'). This fits with the claim that a core life problem for today's young people is precarity. Older people were more persuaded by narrative four. Narrative four combines two main themes: basic income not disincentivising work, and basic income being good for health and wellbeing. Older people may be more concerned about deservingness considerations, and for them it is reassuring that idleness would not be incentivised. Plus, older people in the UK typically have more economic security than younger people: there is a generous and secure state pension, and many of them acquired property earlier in their lives. Where young people worry about lack of economic security, older people worry, understandably, about poor health. We found elsewhere in the study that older people were more receptive to arguments framed around the health benefits of basic income, whereas younger people were more receptive to economic security arguments.

**Opening the Overton window**

The political scientist Joseph Overton introduced the 'Overton window' or 'window of discourse'.[14] This is the range of policies that mainstream political parties are willing to discuss at any point in time. By mainstream, we mean parties that see themselves as having a good chance of capturing power soon. Despite attracting some interest, basic income has been on the outer edge of, or outside, the Overton window in the last few decades. This explains its adoption by smaller parties (who need only appeal to a devoted subgroup), think tanks and academics, coupled with a reluctance to talk about it from mainstream parties. The point about the Overton window is that it moves. It can move quite rapidly. Is the Overton window now moving in such a way as to put basic income inside it?

We believe that it is. Our reasons recapitulate several points we have already made. Act one in a move in the Overton window is the realisation that the status quo is not working, not well enough or for enough people. The failure of the status quo is necessary, but it is not sufficient. There must also be a positive alternative to think about. Act two is enough people coming to believe that a particular reform – in this case basic income – would be better than the status quo, and better by a sufficient margin to make the upheaval worthwhile. In act two, you expect early championing of the reform by smaller political parties and political outsiders, sniffing the opportunity to increase their visibility in the conversation. The survey evidence we have reviewed in this chapter, as well as prominence of basic income in the electoral offer of the Green Party and others, convinces us that act two is well in progress. There is an important moment in act two when citizens realise not just that *they* personally think basic income is a good idea, but that *many other people* do too. This makes them comfortable to talk about it, without worrying that they will meet with incomprehension.

Act three, running somewhat concurrently with act two, involves the development and circulation of compelling argumentative justifications for the reform. Argumentative justification is an expressive activity, and also a skill. You get better and more convincing at it with more practice. Small parties, civic organisations, think tanks and academics can build up the pool of argumentative justifications for a reform, and once those become bulletproof, mainstream politicians start to feel safe coming onside. Sometimes, an authoritative argumentative case comes from outside the political parties altogether. An example was William Beveridge's 1942 report, which produced a blueprint for the postwar UK welfare state. There is a certain point where the accumulated discursive case is so compelling that it becomes more of an argumentative liability *not* to propose the reform than to propose it, and this is when one would expect mainstream parties to move, perhaps quite abruptly. We have shown in this chapter how, when prompted to engage with the idea of basic income, people can come up with argumentative justifications that are highly convincing, perhaps to their own surprise. This reminds us of the importance of social communication, especially between people who do not agree, in democracy.[15]

We are possibly over-optimistic – one should never forget the stickiness of current institutions, and all the reasons for not acting – but we feel that it may not be very long before basic income is firmly visible through the Overton window. Mainstream politicians (like those in the Labour Party) will in a sense be the last to know: for professional reasons they are overly attached to minor skirmishes around incremental solutions they spend their work time tweaking. They are like generals, always fighting the last war, not seeing the landscape currently in front of them. But, they will soon need to exhibit some flexibility and vision, or be swept away. Once a reform is visible through the Overton window, if it is a good one, history shows that it is not very long before the politically possible becomes the politically inevitable.

### Case Study: Changing minds and working for better reasons

For Jane, a health worker in her 60s from Durham, hard work has been central to her life and identity. For decades, she has contributed to our nation's health and been motivated by that commitment to public service as well as by the need to support her family. She is now in a senior managerial position and became eligible for retirement during a period of financial restructuring. Far from giving up work when she was able to do so, she found that her relationship with it changed:

> I could retire whenever I want. That's the first time I've ever been able to do this. But now I feel like I'm working for the right reasons – because I know I can do a good job and play a part in making life better for my colleagues and the people we serve. I want to work and that makes my professional and personal life that much healthier and happier. Work is a central part of who I am and not working out of fear of not having enough has changed the way I think about policies like basic income.

Jane recalled discussions she's had with friends who have voted Conservative in recent years.

> My friends have real concerns about immigration and welfare dependency. I thought that mentioning basic income would just give them ammunition about this, but explaining that everyone who is in Britain legitimately would receive the payment changed how they saw welfare. They could see that it would end the unfairness of people like them not receiving the same support as those who don't work and would enable people to do the things they need to do. Suddenly, they could see that this was a policy for them, not for others, and that changed everything about the way they see basic income. This is the policy for people who want to work.

## If you like basic income, you're in the majority

There is widespread belief across Britain that the distribution of wealth is wrong, and growing support for basic income as a means of correcting that and providing us with the security we need.[16]

## Conclusion

The idea that, by social means, we should provide one another with basic predictability, protection against the worst that may happen, and a stake in the public windfalls of nature and culture, is as old as society itself. In fact, it is the very idea of society. The forms by which societies have realised the imperative have varied through history: from informal sharing, through the commons, seigneurial largesse, private charity, to the different forms of the welfare state. This long-term evolution is to be expected, as societies become more affluent, and people make their livings in different ways. It has not finished.

In this book, we have argued that the right way to fulfil the social imperative, for the UK and other high-income countries in the 21st century, is to introduce basic income. No other institutional form gives the same range of advantages. Basic income targets poverty and reduces inequality. By moving more of people's livelihoods from the uncertain portion of their income stream to the certain portion it reduces uncertainty and hence stress. Relieved of uncertainty, people can take good risks and avoid bad ones; look towards the long term; and look outward to their communities and environments. The positive effects of reduced poverty, reduced stress, the space to care, and a more long-term and outward-looking perspective will propagate through society. They will propagate through families, communities, workplaces, hospitals and government. Basic income is the right reform for the way we live now, and the way we are likely to live in the medium-term future.

Introducing basic income would be expensive, but what is the alternative? The current welfare system is also extremely expensive. It bakes in the structural issues that contribute to our society being so sick. The cost of mopping up the failures of our economic model via the healthcare system, the criminal justice system, the social care system, and so on, outweigh any reasonable advantage from forcing people to comply with conditionality. Many of the things that the state does are expensive: maintaining an army; running a hospital system; and, more controversially, keeping capital markets lubricated through quantitative easing. States do expensive things when the people in power have been persuaded that those things are necessary to the maintenance of a social system. Given all the chaos associated with our current tax and welfare systems, and the likely costs of alternatives, basic income is the least expensive solution and the most likely to produce significant returns on investment. The expensive solution is hanging on to the status quo – we cannot afford *not* to adopt basic income.

As we have shown, a starter basic income can be introduced in the UK with only modest changes to the tax code, in a way that does not involve the government printing or borrowing money. It would therefore not be inflationary. Incrementally, as savings accrue, tax receipts will rise; as new forms of taxation are explored, basic income can rise towards a full minimum income standard. The administrative distance between where the UK is now, and the starter basic income scheme, is not nearly as far as you might think, given how many working-age households already receive Universal Credit or other government support; given the existence of the personal income tax allowance; and given the fact that over-67s already receive something very like basic income; and given that Child Benefit was, prior to the introduction of the high-income charge, something like a basic income for children. Yet, the psychological distance is very great.

The level of public disaffection with the status quo is very high. People of all demographic groups agree that it is not right that, amid historic abundance, inequality should be as great as it is, and deprivation so widespread and so tragic. They see the effects of precarity and want on their friends and family, their neighbours, their communities, and their fellow citizens. They understand it as a failure of the present system that healthy life expectancy is declining. If you think this, then you need to know that others around you do as well. The present mainstream political offering amounts to steadying course and adopting the blind hope that, in some undefined way, things will get better. We all know that this is magical thinking, and hence most of us have very low regard for contemporary politicians.

This broad popular dissatisfaction has existed for a while. The history of ideas shows that it is not enough for an idea to fail. Another idea must present itself as a better alternative. In our politics the neoliberal settlement that started in the 1970s and 1980s has clearly run into existential problems. However, the broad dissatisfaction stemming from this has not quite found a clear positive programme to attach itself to. Seventeen million people voted for Brexit in 2016. Seven years later, only 22 per cent of respondents to a poll thought it had been a good idea.[1] The Conservatives won a clear majority in 2019 and slumped to their lowest number of seats in 2024. The Labour Party won a majority of seats in parliament in 2024, but on a historically low voter turnout. People want something, but they have not been quite sure what it is. It is incumbent on progressive parties to crystallise an alternative settlement, lest they be replaced by much more dangerous visions from the right.

We think that basic income is a feasible centrepiece for a new political settlement. The demand for it could be the mustering point for popular dissatisfaction, and the shared expression of the desire for a better life for all. In its starter form, it is adjacent enough to the status quo as to be feasible, but it is also transformational enough to qualify as a big idea. Our polling evidence shows that basic income is already popular enough for this to start happening. We hope and expect that the process will accelerate, and that momentum will gather. There are basic income conversations, trials, pilots and arguments happening all over the world, with ever greater energy and visibility.[2]

We will end with a reflection on the notion of health. One way in which our case for basic income differs from others that have been made is our emphasis on basic income as an intervention to improve health, and to reverse declines in healthy life expectancy. An organism is, broadly speaking, healthy when it has the resources it needs to fuel its basic functions, and is able to protect itself from environmental perturbations that threaten its integrity. This principle can be applied to mental health as surely as to physical health. Resources are things like food, shelter, clean air and water; and perturbations are things like unemployment, food insecurity, hunger, eviction, violence and family breakdown. Basic income helps with both the resource need and the perturbations. It *resources* people to fulfil their fundamental needs, meaning that extra resources they capture in the marketplace can be used to go beyond the basic and make life richer. It *protects* people from many types of environmental perturbation, by providing an ongoing, certain income stream that they know will be there at the moment they need it.

One of the things we have learned in the last few decades is that the determinants of individual health are, to a very great extent, social. We are creatures of and for society. For individuals to be healthy, they have to be embedded in social networks and institutions that protect and resource them. That is why the right level to tackle worsening population health is institutional reform – introducing basic income – not just medical treatment or individual healthy living advice. But as well as individual health being promoted through societal means, we can speak, in a way that is only slightly figurative, of *society itself* being healthy. Most people agree that there is something sick or ill about societies of historic abundance in which many people cannot access enough to eat; where the degree of inequality is so massive that whole groups of people are effectively dominated by powerful others, and live in fear; and where citizens are turned inwards into themselves, away from the public sphere, through stress and insecurity. Introducing basic income is the crucial step towards making our society healthier.

# Notes

## Introduction

1. G. Standing, *Basic Income: And How We Can Make It Happen* (London: Pelican, 2017); G. Standing, *Battling Eight Giants: Basic Income Now* (London, New York, Oxford, New Delhi and Sydney: I.B. Tauris, 2020).
2. P. Van Parijs and Y. Vanderborght, *Basic Income: A Radical Proposal for a Free Society and a Sane Economy* (Cambridge, MA: Harvard University Press, 2019).
3. M.T. Johnson and E.A. Johnson, 'Examining the Ethical Underpinnings of Universal Basic Income as a Public Health Policy: Prophylaxis, Social Engineering and "Good" Lives', *Journal of Medical Ethics* 47, no. 12 (December 2021): e71–e71, https://doi.org/10.1136/medethics-2020-106477.
4. J. Wright, R. McEachan and M. Mathai, 'Why Is the Born in Bradford Cohort Study Important for Child Health?', *Archives of Disease in Childhood* 107, no. 8 (August 2022): 708–709, https://doi.org/10.1136/archdischild-2020-321231.
5. J. Wright, A.C. Hayward, J. West, K.E. Pickett, R.M. McEachan, M. Mon-Williams, et al, 'ActEarly: A City Collaboratory Approach to Early Promotion of Good Health and Wellbeing', *Wellcome Open Research*, 14 October 2019, https://doi.org/10.12688/wellcomeopenres.15443.1.
6. E.A. Johnson, H. Webster, J. Morrison, R. Thorold, A. Mathers, D. Nettle, et al, 'What Role Do Young People Believe Universal Basic Income Can Play in Supporting Their Mental Health?', *Journal of Youth Studies*, 2023, 1–20, https://doi.org/10.1080/13676261.2023.2256236; N. Howard, E.A. Johnson, G. Gregory, J. Coates, C. Goodman, A. Corrigan, et al, 'Designing Basic Income Pilots for Community Development: What are the Key Community Concerns?', *Local Development and Society*, 2023, https://doi.org/10.1080/26883597.2023.2269483; N. Howard, G. Gregory, E.A. Johnson, J. Coates, C. Goodman, K.E. Pickett, et al, 'The Prospective Health Impacts of a Universal Basic Income: Evidence from Community Engagement in South Tyneside, United Kingdom', *International Journal of Social Determinants of Health and Health Services* 54, no. 4 (October 2024): 396–404, https://doi.org/10.1177/27551938241265928; Northumberland County Council, 'Northumberland County Council: Energising Blyth', accessed 16 May 2024, https://www.northumberland.gov.uk/Economy-Regeneration/Programmes/Town-Centre-Regeneration/Energising-Blyth.aspx.

# Notes

## Chapter 1

1. Office for National Statistics, 'National Life Tables: Life Expectancy in the UK', accessed 14 May 2024, https://www.ons.gov.uk/peoplepopulationandcommunity/birthsdeathsandmarriages/lifeexpectancies/bulletins/nationallifetablesunitedkingdom/2020to2022.
2. Office for National Statistics, 'Average Household Income, UK', accessed 14 May 2024, https://www.ons.gov.uk/peoplepopulationandcommunity/personalandhouseholdfinances/incomeandwealth/bulletins/householddisposableincomeandinequality/financialyearending2022.
3. Ipsos, 'Three in Four Think Britain Is Becoming a Worse Place to Live', 31 July 2023, https://www.ipsos.com/en-uk/three-four-think-britain-becoming-worse-place-live.
4. Office for National Statistics, 'Optimism and Personal Well-Being: Technical Report', accessed 14 May 2024, https://www.ons.gov.uk/peoplepopulationandcommunity/wellbeing/methodologies/optimismandpersonalwellbeingtechnicalreport.
5. C. Archer, K. Turner, D. Kessler, B. Mars and N. Wiles, 'Trends in the Recording of Anxiety in UK Primary Care: A Multi-Method Approach', *Social Psychiatry and Psychiatric Epidemiology* 57, no. 2 (1 February 2022): 375–386, https://doi.org/10.1007/s00127-021-02131-8.
6. F. Parra-Mujica, E. Johnson, H. Reed, R. Cookson and M. Johnson, 'Understanding the Relationship between Income and Mental Health among 16- to 24-Year-Olds: Analysis of 10 Waves (2009–2020) of Understanding Society to Enable Modelling of Income Interventions', *PLoS One* 18, no. 2 (28 February 2023): e0279845, https://doi.org/10.1371/journal.pone.0279845; A. Villadsen, E.A. Johnson, R. Cookson and M. Johnson, 'How Far Can Interventions to Increase Income Improve Adolescent Mental Health? Evidence from the UK Millennium Cohort Study and Next Steps', *Journal of Prevention and Health Promotion* 5 no. 1 (21 March 2024): 153–181, https://doi.org/10.1177/26320770231204993.
7. S. McManus, P. Bebbington, R. Jenkins and T. Brugha (eds), *Mental Health and Wellbeing in England: Adult Psychiatric Morbidity Survey 2014* (Leeds: NHS Digital, 2016), accessed 26 October 2024, https://assets.publishing.service.gov.uk/media/5a802e2fe5274a2e8ab4ea71/apms-2014-full-rpt.pdf.
8. Office for National Statistics, 'National Life Tables: Life Expectancy in the UK'.
9. Office for National Statistics, 'Health State Life Expectancies in England, Northern Ireland and Wales', accessed 14 May 2024, https://www.ons.gov.uk/peoplepopulationandcommunity/healthandsocialcare/healthandlifeexpectancies/bulletins/healthstatelifeexpectanciesuk/between2011to2013and2020to2022.
10. Department for Levelling Up, Housing and Communities, *Levelling Up the United Kingdom: White Paper* (London: HMSO, 2022), accessed 26 October 2024, https://www.gov.uk/government/publications/levelling-up-the-united-kingdom.

11. Office for National Statistics, 'Data on Economic Inactivity Because of Long-Term Sickness', accessed 14 May 2024, https://www.ons.gov.uk/employmentandlabourmarket/peoplenotinwork/economicinactivity/datasets/dataoneconomicactivitybecauseoflongtermsickness.
12. GOV.UK, 'Benefit Expenditure and Caseload Tables 2023', 22 April 2024, https://www.gov.uk/government/publications/benefit-expenditure-and-caseload-tables-2023.
13. GOV.UK, 'Guidance and Methodology: Benefit Expenditure and Caseload Tables', accessed 14 May 2024, https://www.gov.uk/government/publications/benefit-expenditure-and-caseload-tables-information-and-guidance/benefit-expenditure-and-caseload-tables-information-and-guidance.
14. M.T. Johnson and E. Johnson, 'Stress, Domination and Basic Income: Considering a Citizens' Entitlement Response to a Public Health Crisis', *Social Theory & Health* 17, no. 2 (June 2019): 253–271, https://doi.org/10.1057/s41285-018-0076-3.
15. J.M. Keynes, *Essays in Persuasion* (New York: Norton, 1963).
16. Office for National Statistics, 'UK Measures of National Well-Being Dashboard', accessed 14 May 2024, https://www.ons.gov.uk/peoplepopulationandcommunity/wellbeing/articles/ukmeasuresofnationalwellbeing/dashboard.
17. Food Foundation, 'Food Insecurity Tracking', accessed 14 May 2024, https://foodfoundation.org.uk/initiatives/food-insecurity-tracking.
18. T. Piketty, *Capital in the Twenty-First Century* (Cambridge, MA: Harvard University Press, 2013).
19. L. Calafati, J. Froud, C. Haslam, S. Johal and K. Williams, *When Nothing Works: From Cost of Living to Foundational Liveability* (Manchester: Manchester University Press, 2023).
20. *The Baffler*, 'Of Flying Cars and the Declining Rate of Profit', accessed 14 May 2024, https://thebaffler.com/salvos/of-flying-cars-and-the-declining-rate-of-profit.
21. Office for National Statistics, 'UK Measures of National Well-Being Dashboard'.
22. P. Turchin, *End Times: Elites, Counter-Elites and the Path of Political Disintegration* (London: Penguin, 2023); T. Gurr, *Why Men Rebel* (Oxford: Routledge, 2011).
23. N. Howard, G. Gregory, E.A. Johnson, C. Goodman, J. Coates, I. Robson, et al, 'Designing Basic Income Pilots for Community Development: What Are the Key Community Concerns? Evidence from Citizen Engagement in Northern England', *Local Development & Society*, 11 October 2023, 1–17, https://doi.org/10.1080/26883597.2023.2269483.
24. D. Degerman, E. Johnson, M. Flinders and M. Johnson, 'After Nudging: The Ethical Challenge of Post-Pandemic Policymaking in the UK', *Humanities and Social Sciences Communications* 11, no. 1 (29 March 2024): 1–9, https://doi.org/10.1057/s41599-024-02980-z.
25. A. Villadsen, E.A. Johnson, R. Cookson and M.T. Johnson, 'How Far Can Interventions to Increase Income Improve Adolescent Mental Health?

## Notes

Evidence From the UK Millennium Cohort Study and Next Steps', *Journal of Prevention and Health Promotion* 5, no. 1 (1 January 2024): 153–181, https://doi.org/10.1177/26320770231204993.

26. G. Standing, *The Precariat: The New Dangerous Class* (London: Bloomsbury, 2011).
27. R.D. Brown and G.V. Pepper, 'The Uncontrollable Mortality Risk Hypothesis: Theoretical Foundations and Implications for Public Health', *Evolution, Medicine, and Public Health*, 12, no. 1 (2024): 86–96, https://doi.org/10.1093/emph/eoae009.
28. M.T. Johnson, E.A. Johnson, D. Nettle and K.E. Pickett, 'Designing Trials of Universal Basic Income for Health Impact: Identifying Interdisciplinary Questions to Address', *Journal of Public Health* 44, no. 2 (27 June 2022): 408–416, https://doi.org/10.1093/pubmed/fdaa255; M.T. Johnson, E.A. Johnson and K.E. Pickett, 'The Health Case for Universal Basic Income', in *The Palgrave International Handbook of Basic Income*, ed. M. Torry, 2nd edn (Cham: Springer International Publishing, 2023), 109–130; E.A. Johnson, M.T. Johnson, C. Kypridemos, A. Villadsen and K.E. Pickett, 'Designing a Generic, Adaptive Protocol Resource for the Measurement of Health Impact in Cash Transfer Pilot and Feasibility Studies and Trials in High-Income Countries', *Pilot and Feasibility Studies* 9, no. 1 (23 March 2023): Article 51, https://doi.org/10.1186/s40814-023-01276-4.
29. D. Nettle, C. Chevallier, B. de Courson, E.A. Johnson, M.T. Johnson and K.E. Pickett, 'Short-Term Changes in Financial Situation Have Immediate Mental Health Consequences: Implications for Social Policy', *Social Policy & Administration*, 21 July 2024, https://doi.org/10.1111/spol.13065.
30. Wickham, S., Bentley, L., Rose, T., Whitehead, M., Taylor-Robinson, D. and Barr, B. (2020). Effects on mental health of a UK welfare reform, Universal Credit: A longitudinal controlled study. *The Lancet Public Health*, 5(3), e157–e164. https://doi.org/10.1016/S2468-2667(20)30026-8
31. H.R. Reed, M.T. Johnson, S. Lansley, E.A. Johnson, G. Stark and K.E. Pickett, 'Universal Basic Income Is Affordable and Feasible: Evidence from UK Economic Microsimulation Modelling', *Journal of Poverty and Social Justice* 31, no. 1 (February 2023): 146–162, https://doi.org/10.1332/175982721X16702368352393.
32. M. Gibson, W. Hearty and P. Craig, 'The Public Health Effects of Interventions Similar to Basic Income: A Scoping Review', *The Lancet Public Health* 5, no. 3 (1 March 2020): e165–e176, https://doi.org/10.1016/S2468-2667(20)30005-0.
33. T. Chen, H. Reed, F. Parra-Mujica, E.A. Johnson, M. Johnson, M. O'Flaherty, et al, 'Quantifying the Mental Health and Economic Impacts of Prospective Universal Basic Income Schemes among Young People in the UK: A Microsimulation Modelling Study', *BMJ Open* 13, no. 10 (1 October 2023): e075831, https://doi.org/10.1136/bmjopen-2023-075831.
34. Common Sense Policy Group, *Act Now. A Vision for a Better Future and a New Social Contract* (Manchester: Manchester University Press, 2024).

35 Institute for Government, 'Civil Service Staff Numbers', accessed 14 May 2024, https://www.instituteforgovernment.org.uk/explainer/civil-service-staff-numbers.

36 GOV.UK, 'Quarterly Service Personnel Statistics 1 October 2023', accessed 14 May 2024, https://www.gov.uk/government/statistics/quarterly-service-personnel-statistics-2023/quarterly-service-personnel-statistics-1-october-2023.

37 E. Kirk-Wade, 'Reducing the Universal Credit Taper Rate and the Effect on Incomes', 1 February 2022, https://commonslibrary.parliament.uk/reducing-the-universal-credit-taper-rate-and-the-effect-on-incomes/.

38 E. Johnson and E. Spring, 'The Activity Trap', Activity Alliance, 10 October 2018, http://www.activityalliance.org.uk/assets/000/002/433/Activity_Alliance_-_The_Activity_Trap_full_report_Accessible_PDF_FINAL_original.pdf?1538668349.

39 Johnson and Spring, 'The Activity Trap'.

40 Joseph Rowntree Foundation, 'UK Poverty 2023: The Essential Guide to Understanding Poverty in the UK', 26 January 2023, https://www.jrf.org.uk/uk-poverty-2023-the-essential-guide-to-understanding-poverty-in-the-uk.

41 GOV.UK, 'Universal Credit: 29 April 2013 to 13 July 2023', accessed 14 May 2024, https://www.gov.uk/government/statistics/universal-credit-statistics-29-april-2013-to-13-july-2023/universal-credit-29-april-2013-to-13-july-2023.

42 Van Parijs and Vanderborght, *Basic Income*.

43 I. Marinescu, 'No Strings Attached: The Behavioral Effects of U.S. Unconditional Cash Transfer Programs', National Bureau of Economic Research, February 2018, https://doi.org/10.3386/w24337; U. Huws, M. Torry and G. Yi, 'Employment Market Effects of Basic Income', in *The Palgrave International Handbook of Basic Income*, ed. M. Torry, 2nd edn (Cham: Springer International Publishing, 2023), 63–90, https://doi.org/10.1007/978-3-031-41001-7_4.

44 R.D. Arvey, I. Harpaz and H. Liao, 'Work Centrality and Post-Award Work Behavior of Lottery Winners', *The Journal of Psychology* 138, no. 5 (1 September 2004): 404–420, https://doi.org/10.3200/JRLP.138.5.404-420.

45 Marinescu, 'No Strings Attached'; P. Knight, 'UBI: Short-Term Results from a Long-Term Experiment in Kenya', BIEN – Basic Income Earth Network, 19 December 2023, https://basicincome.org/news/2023/12/ubi-short-term-results-from-a-long-term-experiment-in-kenya/.

46 E. Lawlor, H. Kersley and S. Steed, 'A Bit Rich', New Economics Foundation, 14 December 2009, accessed 16 May 2024, https://neweconomics.org/2009/12/a-bit-rich.

47 D. Nettle, K. Panchanathan, T.S. Rai and A.P. Fiske, 'The Evolution of Giving, Sharing, and Lotteries', *Current Anthropology* 52, no 5 (2011): 747–756, accessed 14 May 2024, https://doi.org/10.1086/661521; A.P. Fiske, *Structures of Social Life: The Four Elementary Forms of Human Relations* (New York: Free Press, 1991).

# Notes

48  M. Thatcher, 'Speech to the Institute of SocioEconomic Studies ("Let Our Children Grow Tall")', Margaret Thatcher Foundation, accessed 16 May 2024, https://www.margaretthatcher.org/document/102769.
49  S. Birnbaum, 'The Ethics of Basic Income', in *The Palgrave International Handbook of Basic Income*, ed. M. Torry, 2nd edn (Cham: Springer International Publishing, 2023), 581–596, https://doi.org/10.1007/978-3-031-41001-7_29.
50  E.J. Costello, A. Erkanli, W. Copeland and A. Angold, 'Association of Family Income Supplements in Adolescence With Development of Psychiatric and Substance Use Disorders in Adulthood Among an American Indian Population', *JAMA* 303, no. 19 (19 May 2010): 1954–1960, https://doi.org/10.1001/jama.2010.621; D.K. Evans and A. Popova, 'Cash Transfers and Temptation Goods', *Economic Development and Cultural Change* 65, no. 2 (January 2017): 189–221, https://doi.org/10.1086/689575.
51  T.A. Bruckner, R.A. Brown and C. Margerison-Zilko, 'Positive Income Shocks and Accidental Deaths among Cherokee Indians: A Natural Experiment', *International Journal of Epidemiology* 40, no. 4 (1 August 2011): 1083–1090, https://doi.org/10.1093/ije/dyr073.
52  C.J. Katz, 'Thomas Jefferson's Liberal Anticapitalism', *American Journal of Political Science* 47, no. 1 (2003): 1–17, https://doi.org/10.1111/1540-5907.00001.
53  P. Pettit, *Just Freedom: A Moral Compass for a Complex World* (New York: W.W. Norton & Company, 2014).
54  P. Jones, 'Bearing the Consequences of Belief', *Journal of Political Philosophy* 2, no. 1 (1994): 24–43, accessed 25 May 2024, https://doi.org/10.1111/j.1467-9760.1994.tb00014.x.
55  J. Preiss, 'Why Friedman's Free Market Needs Basic Income', *IAI News*, 14 April 2023, accessed 26 October 2024, https://iai.tv/articles/why-friedmans-free-market-needs-basic-income-joshua-preiss-auid-2452.
56  F. Hayek, *Law, Legislation and Liberty*, vol. 3 (Chicago: University of Chicago Press, 1979), 55.
57  J. Burn-Murdoch, 'Britain and the US Are Poor Societies with Some Very Rich People', *Financial Times*, 16 September 2022, accessed 26 May 2024, https://www.ft.com/content/ef265420-45e8-497b-b308-c951baa68945.

## Chapter 2

1  Reed et al, 'Universal Basic Income Is Affordable and Feasible'.
2  https://ifs.org.uk/tools_and_resources/where_do_you_fit_in.
3  G. Charness and M. Rabin, 'Understanding Social Preferences with Simple Tests', *The Quarterly Journal of Economics* 117, no. 3 (2002): 817–869, accessed 16 May 2024, https://doi.org/10.1162/003355302760193904; T. Kameda, K. Inukai, S. Higuchi, A. Ogawa, H. Kim, T. Matsuda, et al, 'Rawlsian Maximin Rule Operates as a Common Cognitive Anchor in Distributive Justice and Risky Decisions', *Proceedings of the National Academy of Sciences* 113, no. 42 (18 October 2016): 11817–11822, https://doi.org/10.1073/pnas.1602641113; D. Nettle, J. Chrisp, E. Johnson and M.T. Johnson, 'What

Do People Want from a Welfare System? Conjoint Survey Evidence from UK Adults', Working Paper, 21 September 2023, https://doi.org/10.31235/osf.io/zfnuh.

4   Reed et al, 'Universal Basic Income Is Affordable and Feasible'.

5   Our World in Data, 'Income Inequality: Gini Coefficient', accessed 16 May 2024, https://ourworldindata.org/grapher/economic-inequality-gini-index?tab=table.

6   Institute for Fiscal Studies, 'Living Standards, Poverty and Inequality in the UK', n.d., accessed 21 March 2024, https://ifs.org.uk/living-standards-poverty-and-inequality-uk.

7   D. Brady, 'Poverty, Not the Poor', *Science Advances* 9, no. 34 (2023), accessed 16 May 2024, https://www.science.org/doi/10.1126/sciadv.adg1469.

8   J.B. Dowd, J. Albright, T.E. Raghunathan, R.F. Schoeni, F. LeClere and G.A. Kaplan, 'Deeper and Wider: Income and Mortality in the USA over Three Decades', *International Journal of Epidemiology* 40, no. 1 (2011): 183–188, accessed 16 May 2024, https://doi.org/10.1093/ije/dyq189.

9   K. Barnett, S.W. Mercer, M. Norbury, G. Watt, S. Wyke and B. Guthrie, 'Epidemiology of Multimorbidity and Implications for Health Care, Research, and Medical Education: A Cross-Sectional Study', *The Lancet* 380, no. 9836 (2012): 37–43, accessed 16 May 2024, https://doi.org/10.1016/S0140-6736(12)60240-2.

10  P. Cuijpers and F. Smit, 'Excess Mortality in Depression: A Meta-Analysis of Community Studies', *Journal of Affective Disorders* 72, no. 3 (1 December 2002): 227–236, https://doi.org/10.1016/S0165-0327(01)00413-X.

11  L. Akanni, O. Lenhart and A. Morton, 'Income Trajectories and Self-Rated Health Status in the UK', *SSM – Population Health* 17 (March 2022): 101035, https://doi.org/10.1016/j.ssmph.2022.101035; R.M. Thomson, E. Igelström, A.K. Purba, M. Shimonovich, H. Thomson, G. McCartney, et al, 'How Do Income Changes Impact on Mental Health and Wellbeing for Working-Age Adults? A Systematic Review and Meta-Analysis', *The Lancet Public Health* 7, no. 6 (June 2022): e515–528, https://doi.org/10.1016/S2468-2667(22)00058-5.

12  Nettle et al, 'Short-Term Changes in Financial Situation'.

13  H. Reed, E.A. Johnson, G. Stark, D. Nettle, K.E. Pickett and M.T. Johnson, 'Estimating the Effects of Basic Income Schemes on Mental and Physical Health Among Adults Aged 18 and Above in the UK: A Microsimulation Study', *PLoS Mental Health* 1, no. 7 (December 2024), https://doi.org/10.1371/journal.pmen.0000206.

14  N. Krieger, D.H. Rehkopf, J.T. Chen, P.D. Waterman, E. Marcelli and M. Kennedy, 'The Fall and Rise of US Inequities in Premature Mortality: 1960–2002', *PLoS Medicine* 5, no. 2 (26 February 2008): e46, https://doi.org/10.1371/journal.pmed.0050046; C. Shaw, T. Blakely, J. Atkinson and P. Crampton, 'Do Social and Economic Reforms Change Socioeconomic Inequalities in Child Mortality? A Case Study: New Zealand 1981–1999', *Journal of Epidemiology & Community Health* 59, no. 8 (1 August 2005): 638–644, https://doi.org/10.1136/jech.2004.032466; C.L. Niedzwiedz,

# Notes

R.J. Mitchell, N.K. Shortt and J.R. Pearce, 'Social Protection Spending and Inequalities in Depressive Symptoms across Europe', *Social Psychiatry and Psychiatric Epidemiology* 51 (2016): 1005–1014, https://doi.org/10.1007/s00127-016-1223-6.

15  C. Bambra, 'Levelling Up: Global Examples of Reducing Health Inequalities', *Scandinavian Journal of Public Health*, 50, no. 7 (2022): 908–913, https://doi.org/10.1177/14034948211022428.

16  E.L. Forget, 'The Town with No Poverty: The Health Effects of a Canadian Guaranteed Annual Income Field Experiment', *Canadian Public Policy* 37, no. 3 (1 September 2011): 283–305, https://doi.org/10.3138/cpp.37.3.283.

17  F. Pega, R. Pabayo, C. Benny, E.-Y. Lee, S.K. Lhachimi and S.Y. Liu, 'Unconditional Cash Transfers for Reducing Poverty and Vulnerabilities: Effect on Use of Health Services and Health Outcomes in Low- and Middle-income Countries', *Cochrane Database of Systematic Reviews* 3, no. CD011135 (2022), https://doi.org/10.1002/14651858.cd011135.pub3.

18  J. McGuire, C. Kaiser and A.M. Bach-Mortensen, 'A Systematic Review and Meta-Analysis of the Impact of Cash Transfers on Subjective Well-Being and Mental Health in Low- and Middle-Income Countries', *Nature Human Behaviour* 6, no. 3 (March 2022): 359–370, https://doi.org/10.1038/s41562-021-01252-z; M. Ridley, G. Rao, F. Schilbach and V. Patel, 'Poverty, Depression, and Anxiety: Causal Evidence and Mechanisms', *Science* 370, no. 6522 (11 December 2020): eaay0214, https://doi.org/10.1126/science.aay0214.

19  Reed et al, 'Estimating the Effects of Basic Income Schemes'.

20  *Northumberland Gazette*, 'The 20 Poorest Neighbourhoods in Northumberland Based on Average Income Including Parts of Alnwick, Ashington, Berwick, Morpeth and Blyth', 25 January 2023, accessed 26 October 2024, https://www.northumberlandgazette.co.uk/news/people/the-20-poorest-neighbourhoods-in-northumberland-based-on-average-income-including-parts-of-alnwick-ashington-berwick-morpeth-and-blyth-4001035; Northumberland County Council, 'Northumberland County Council: Area Classifications & Indices of Deprivation', accessed 16 May 2024, https://www.northumberland.gov.uk/Northumberland-Knowledge/Our-Community-and-Place/Classifications.aspx.

21  *The Times*, 'Harsh Words in Blyth, the Town That Levelling up Forgot', accessed 16 May 2024, https://www.thetimes.co.uk/article/harsh-words-in-blyth-the-town-that-levelling-up-forgot-x5xh3tz8k.

22  *Chronicle Live*, 'Fears Blyth Could Become "Ghost Town" after Keel Row Shopping Centre Closes Down', accessed 16 May 2024, https://www.chroniclelive.co.uk/news/north-east-news/keel-row-closure-blyth-northumberland-28399871?utm_source=mynewsassistant.com&utm_medium=referral&utm_campaign=embedded_search_item_desktop.

## Chapter 3

1  Ciphr, 'Workplace Stress Statistics in the UK', 31 August 2021, https://www.ciphr.com/infographics/workplace-stress-statistics.

2   L. Macchia and A.J. Oswald, 'National Worry and the Psychological Value of the Welfare State', 2024, accessed 26 October 2024, https://www.andrewoswald.com/docs/Rev-Macchia-Oswald-worry-and-welfare-state-paper-March2024.pdf.
3   J. Wang, 'Work Stress as a Risk Factor for Major Depressive Episode(s)', *Psychological Medicine* 35, no. 6 (June 2005): 865–871, https://doi.org/10.1017/S0033291704003241; J.E.B. van der Waerden, C. Hoefnagels, C.M.H. Hosman and M.W.J. Jansen, 'Defining Subgroups of Low Socioeconomic Status Women at Risk for Depressive Symptoms: The Importance of Perceived Stress and Cumulative Risks', *International Journal of Social Psychiatry* 60, no. 8 (1 December 2014): 772–782, https://doi.org/10.1177/0020764014522751.
4   B Öhlin, P.M. Nilsson, J.-Å. Nilsson and G. Berglund, 'Chronic Psychosocial Stress Predicts Long-Term Cardiovascular Morbidity and Mortality in Middle-Aged Men', *European Heart Journal* 25, no. 10 (1 May 2004): 867–873, https://doi.org/10.1016/j.ehj.2004.03.003; N.R. Nielsen, T.S. Kristensen, P. Schnohr and M. Grønbaek, 'Perceived Stress and Cause-Specific Mortality among Men and Women: Results from a Prospective Cohort Study', *American Journal of Epidemiology* 168, no. 5 (1 September 2008): 481–491, https://doi.org/10.1093/aje/kwn157.
5   L. Prior, D. Manley and K. Jones, 'Stressed Out? An Investigation of Whether Allostatic Load Mediates Associations between Neighbourhood Deprivation and Health', *Health & Place* 52 (July 2018): 25–33, https://doi.org/10.1016/j.healthplace.2018.05.003; P.M. Lantz, J.S. House, R.P. Mero and D.R. Williams, 'Stress, Life Events, and Socioeconomic Disparities in Health: Results from the Americans' Changing Lives Study', *Journal of Health and Social Behavior* 46, no. 3 (1 September 2005): 274–288, https://doi.org/10.1177/002214650504600305; S. Cohen and D. Janicki-Deverts, 'Who's Stressed? Distributions of Psychological Stress in the United States in Probability Samples from 1983, 2006, and 2009', *Journal of Applied Social Psychology* 42, no. 6 (2012): 1320–1334, accessed 16 May 2024, https://doi.org/10.1111/j.1559-1816.2012.00900.x.
6   B. Jimeno and S. Verhulst, 'Meta-Analysis Reveals Glucocorticoid Levels Reflect Variation in Metabolic Rate, Not "Stress"', *eLife* 12 (27 October 2023): RP88205, https://doi.org/10.7554/eLife.88205.
7   Öhlin et al, 'Chronic Psychosocial Stress'; S. Cohen, D. Janicki-Deverts, W.J. Doyle, G.E. Miller, E. Frank, B.S. Rabin, et al, 'Chronic Stress, Glucocorticoid Receptor Resistance, Inflammation, and Disease Risk', *Proceedings of the National Academy of Sciences* 109, no. 16 (17 April 2012): 5995–5999, https://doi.org/10.1073/pnas.1118355109; C. Hammen, E.Y. Kim, N.K. Eberhart and P.A. Brennan, 'Chronic and Acute Stress and the Prediction of Major Depression in Women', *Depression and Anxiety*, 3 June 2009, accessed 25 May 2024, https://doi.org/10.1002/da.20571.
8   A.O. de Berker, R.B. Rutledge, C. Mathys, L. Marshall, G.F. Cross, R.J. Dolan, et al, 'Computations of Uncertainty Mediate Acute Stress Responses

## Notes

in Humans', *Nature Communications* 7, no. 1 (29 March 2016): 10996, https://doi.org/10.1038/ncomms10996.

9   L.A. Pervin, 'The Need to Predict and Control under Conditions of Threat', *Journal of Personality*, 31, no. 4 (1963): 570–587, https://doi.org/10.1111/j.1467-6494.1963.tb01320.x; J.M. Weiss, 'Effects of Coping Behavior in Different Warning Signal Conditions on Stress Pathology in Rats', *Journal of Comparative and Physiological Psychology* 77, no. 1 (1971): 1–13, https://doi.org/10.1037/h0031583; E.-M. Seidel, D.M. Pfabigan, A. Hahn, R. Sladky, A. Grahl, K. Paul, et al, 'Uncertainty during Pain Anticipation: The Adaptive Value of Preparatory Processes', *Human Brain Mapping* 36, no. 2 (16 October 2014): 744–755, https://doi.org/10.1002/hbm.22661; W. Yoshida, B. Seymour, M. Koltzenburg and R.J. Dolan, 'Uncertainty Increases Pain: Evidence for a Novel Mechanism of Pain Modulation Involving the Periaqueductal Gray', *Journal of Neuroscience* 33, no. 13 (27 March 2013): 5638–5646, https://doi.org/10.1523/JNEUROSCI.4984-12.2013.

10  A. Peters, B.S. McEwen and K. Friston, 'Uncertainty and Stress: Why It Causes Diseases and How It Is Mastered by the Brain', *Progress in Neurobiology* 156 (1 September 2017): 164–188, https://doi.org/10.1016/j.pneurobio.2017.05.004.

11  C.A. Holt and S.K. Laury, 'Risk Aversion and Incentive Effects', *American Economic Review* 92, no. 5 (December 2002): 1644–1655, https://doi.org/10.1257/000282802762024700; C. Camerer and M. Weber, 'Recent Developments in Modeling Preferences: Uncertainty and Ambiguity', *Journal of Risk and Uncertainty* 5, no. 4 (1 October 1992): 325–370, https://doi.org/10.1007/BF00122575.

12  A.A. Budak, R. Florisson, A. Martin and G. Williams, 'Zero Choices: Swapping Zero-Hour Contracts for Secure, Flexible Working', 20 March 2024, accessed 26 October 2024, https://www.lancaster.ac.uk/workfoundation/publications/zero-choices; G. Giupponi and X. Xu, 'What Does the Rise of Self-Employment Tell Us about the UK Labour Market?', 19 November 2020, accessed 26 October 2024, https://ifs.org.uk/publications/what-does-rise-self-employment-tell-us-about-uk-labour-market.

13  Standing, *The Precariat*.

14  G.M. Sayre, 'The Costs of Insecurity: Pay Volatility and Health Outcomes', *Journal of Applied Psychology* 108, no. 7 (2023): 1223–1243, https://doi.org/10.1037/apl0001062; Akanni et al, 'Income Trajectories and Self-Rated Health Status in the UK'; A. Adeline, I.C. Crevecoeur, R. Fonseca and P.-C. Michaud, 'Income Volatility, Health and Well-Being', IZA Discussion Paper No. 12823, 16 December 2019, https://doi.org/10.2139/ssrn.3503773.

15  Macchia and Oswald, 'National Worry and the Psychological Value of the Welfare State'.

16  Pettit, *Just Freedom*.

17  A.V. Banerjee and E. Duflo, *Good Economics for Bad Times* (London: Allen Lane, 2019).

[18] D. Nettle and R. Saxe, 'Preferences for Redistribution Are Sensitive to Perceived Luck, Social Homogeneity, War and Scarcity', *Cognition* 198 (1 May 2020): 104234, https://doi.org/10.1016/j.cognition.2020.104234; Nettle et al, 'What Do People Want from a Welfare System?'.

[19] D. Nettle, E. Johnson, M. Johnson and R. Saxe, 'Why Has the COVID-19 Pandemic Increased Support for Universal Basic Income?', *Humanities and Social Sciences Communications* 8, no. 1 (December 2021): Article 79, https://doi.org/10.1057/s41599-021-00760-7.

[20] ONS, 'What Are the Regional Differences in Income and Productivity?', accessed 17 May 2024, https://www.ons.gov.uk/visualisations/dvc1370/; ONS, 'Income Estimates for Small Areas, England and Wales', accessed 17 May 2024, https://www.ons.gov.uk/peoplepopulationandcommunity/personalandhouseholdfinances/incomeandwealth/bulletins/smallareamodelbasedincomeestimates/financialyearending2020; 'Report', North East Evidence Hub, accessed 17 May 2024, https://evidencehub.northeast-ca.gov.uk/report.

[21] GOV.UK, 'Personal Tax Credits: Children in Low-Income Families Local Measure: 2014 Snapshot as at 31 August 2014: 30 September 2016', accessed 17 May 2024, https://www.gov.uk/government/statistics/personal-tax-credits-children-in-low-income-families-local-measure-2014-snapshot-as-at-31-august-2014-30-september-2016.

## Chapter 4

[1] Brady, 'Poverty, Not the Poor'.
[2] Bambra, 'Levelling Up'.
[3] Macchia and Oswald, 'National Worry and the Psychological Value of the Welfare State'.
[4] R.D. Brown and G.V. Pepper, 'The Uncontrollable Mortality Risk Hypothesis: Theoretical Foundations and Implications for Public Health', *Evolution, Medicine, and Public Health* 12, no. 1 (2024): 86–96, https://doi.org/10.1093/emph/eoae009.
[5] J. Haushofer and D. Salicath, 'The Psychology of Poverty: Where Do We Stand?', *Social Philosophy and Policy* 40, no. 1 (2023): 150–184, https://doi.org/10.1017/S0265052523000419; Nettle et al, 'Short-Term Changes in Financial Situation'.
[6] M. Johnson, D. Degerman and R. Geyer, 'Exploring the Health Case for Universal Basic Income: Evidence from GPs Working with Precarious Groups', *Basic Income Studies* 14, no. 2 (26 November 2019), https://doi.org/10.1515/bis-2019-0008.
[7] G.V. Pepper and D. Nettle, 'The Behavioural Constellation of Deprivation: Causes and Consequences', *Behavioral and Brain Sciences* 40 (2017): e314, https://doi.org/10.1017/S0140525X1600234X.
[8] R. Brown, E. Sillence and G. Pepper, 'Perceptions of Control over Different Causes of Death and the Accuracy of Risk Estimations', *Journal of Public Health* 32 (14 April 2023): 1271–1284, https://doi.org/10.1007/s10389-023-01910-8; R. Brown and G. Pepper, 'The Relationship Between

# Notes

Perceived Uncontrollable Mortality Risk and Health Effort: Replication, Secondary Analysis, and Mini Meta-Analysis', *Annals of Behavioral Medicine* 58, no. 3 (1 March 2024): 192–204, https://doi.org/10.1093/abm/kaad072.

9   P. Singh, R. Brown, W.E. Copeland, E.J. Costello and T.A. Bruckner, 'Income Dividends and Subjective Survival in a Cherokee Indian Cohort: A Quasi-Experiment', *Biodemography and Social Biology* 65, no. 2 (1 April 2020): 172–187, https://doi.org/10.1080/19485565.2020.1730155.

10  B. de Courson, W. Frankenhuis and D. Nettle, 'Poverty Is Associated with Both Risk Avoidance and Risk Taking: An Empirical Test of the Desperation Threshold Model', SocArXiv, 9 February 2024, https://doi.org/10.31235/osf.io/gqjkm.

11  B. de Courson and D. Nettle, 'Why Do Inequality and Deprivation Produce High Crime and Low Trust?', *Scientific Reports* 11, no. 1 (21 January 2021): Article 1937, https://doi.org/10.1038/s41598-020-80897-8.

12  M. Kelly, 'Inequality and Crime', *The Review of Economics and Statistics* 82, no. 4 (1 November 2000): 530–539, https://doi.org/10.1162/003465300559028; S. Machin and C. Meghir, 'Crime and Economic Incentives', *The Journal of Human Resources* 39, no. 4 (2004): 958–979, https://doi.org/10.2307/3559034; S. Raphael and R. Winter-Ebmer, 'Identifying the Effect of Unemployment on Crime', *The Journal of Law and Economics* 44, no. 1 (April 2001): 259–283, https://doi.org/10.1086/320275.

13  B.A. Jacobs and R. Wright, 'Stick-up, Street Culture, and Offender Motivation', *Criminology* 37, no. 1 (1999): 149–174, https://doi.org/10.1111/j.1745-9125.1999.tb00482.x.

14  Standing, *The Precariat*.

15  M. Duque and A. McKnight, 'Understanding the Relationship between Inequalities and Poverty: Mechanisms Associated with Crime, the Legal System and Punitive Sanctions', London School of Economics: Centre for the Analysis of Social Exclusion, CASE paper 215/LIP paper 6 (2019), accessed 26 October 2024, https://sticerd.lse.ac.uk/dps/case/cp/casepaper215.pdf.

16  CrimeRate, 'UK Crime and Safety Statistics', accessed 21 May 2024, https://crimerate.co.uk/.

17  M. Lindsay, '"Feral" Teens in Masks Terrorising Communities', *BBC News*, 7 March 2024, accessed 21 May 2024, https://www.bbc.co.uk/news/articles/c2v9e1n4q8lo.

18  Northumbria Connected, 'Home Page', accessed 21 May 2024, https://northumbriaconnected.co.uk/.

## Chapter 5

1   United Nations Children's Fund, 'The State of the World's Children 2023: Statistical Tables – Table 2: Child Mortality', UNICEF Innocenti – Global Office of Research and Foresight, 2023, accessed 26 October 2024, https://data.unicef.org/wp-content/uploads/2023/04/Table-2-Child-mortality-SOWC2023.xlsx.

2. A. Gromada, G. Rees and Y. Chzhen, 'Worlds of Influence: Understanding What Shapes Child Well-Being in Rich Countries', Innocenti Report Card, no 16, UNICEF Office of Research, 2020.
3. Department for Work and Pensions, 'Family Resources Survey 2022/23: Disability Data Tables', 21 March 2024, accessed 26 October 2024, https://assets.publishing.service.gov.uk/media/65f0363a981227001af612bc/c4-disability.xlsx.
4. B. Francis-Devine, 'Poverty in the UK: Statistics', House of Commons Library, 8 April 2024, accessed 26 October 2024, https://commonslibrary.parliament.uk/research-briefings/sn07096/.
5. M. Brewer, E. Fry and L. Try, 'The Living Standards Outlook 2023', Resolution Foundation, 9 January 2023, accessed 26 October, https://www.resolutionfoundation.org/publications/the-living-standards-outlook-2023/.
6. F. Hobson, 'The Impact of the Two-Child Limit in Universal Credit', House of Commons Library, 14 February 2024, accessed 26 October 2024, https://researchbriefings.files.parliament.uk/documents/CBP-9301/CBP-9301.pdf.
7. World Bank, 'GDP (Current US$)', The World Bank Data, 28 May 2024, accessed 26 October, https://data.worldbank.org/indicator/NY.GDP.MKTP.CD?most_recent_value_desc=true&year_high_desc=true.
8. S. Wickham, E. Anwar, B. Barr, C. Law and D. Taylor-Robinson, 'Poverty and Child Health in the UK: Using Evidence for Action', *Archives of Disease in Childhood* 101, no. 8 (2016): 759–766, https://doi.org/10.1136/archdischild-2014-306746; R. Atkins, L. Munford and C. Bambra, 'The Economic Impacts of Child Health', in *Child of the North: Building a Fairer Future after COVID-19*, ed. K. Pickett, D. Taylor-Robinson, et al (Northern Health Sciences Alliance & N8 Research Partnership, 2021), 56–60.
9. HM Government, 'An Evidence Review of the Drivers of Child Poverty for Families in Poverty Now and for Poor Children Growing up to Be Poor Adults', Her Majesty's Stationery Office, January 2014, accessed 26 October 2024, https://assets.publishing.service.gov.uk/media/5a7ca9e640f0b65b3de0a616/Cm_8781_Child_Poverty_Evidence_Review_Print.pdf.
10. L. Hodges, S. Shorto and E. Goddard, 'Childcare Survey 2024', Coram Family and Childcare, 2024, accessed 26 October 2024, https://www.familyandchildcaretrust.org/childcare-survey-2024.
11. OECD, 'Net Childcare Costs (Indicator)', 2024, accessed 26 October 2024, https://doi.org/10.1787/e328a9ee-en.
12. Pregnant Then Screwed, 'New Pregnant Then Screwed Data Shows Three-Quarters of Mothers Who Pay for Childcare Say That It Does Not Make Financial Sense for Them to Work', 2 March 2023, accessed 26 October 2024, https://pregnantthenscrewed.com/three-quarters-of-mothers-who-pay-for-childcare-say-that-it-does-not-make-financial-sense-for-them-to-work/.
13. Pregnant Then Screwed, 'Childcare Cost Crisis Persists, despite New Government Funding', 25 March 2024, accessed 26 October 2024, https://pregnantthenscrewed.com/childcare-cost-crisis-persists-despite-new-government-funding/.

# Notes

14. Hodges et al, 'Childcare Survey 2024'.
15. Office for National Statistics, 'Earnings and Hours Worked, Care Workers: ASHE Table 26 – 2023 Provisional Edition of This Dataset', 1 November 2023, accessed 26 October 2024, https://www.ons.gov.uk/employmentandlabourmarket/peopleinwork/earningsandworkinghours/datasets/careworkerssocashetable26.
16. Francis-Devine, 'Poverty in the UK'.
17. TUC, '1 in 4 Children with Care Worker Parents Are Growing up in Poverty', 2 November 2022, accessed 26 October 2024, https://www.tuc.org.uk/news/1-4-children-care-worker-parents-are-growing-poverty.
18. Office for National Statistics, 'Births in England and Wales', 23 February 2024, accessed 26 October 2024, https://www.ons.gov.uk/peoplepopulationandcommunity/birthsdeathsandmarriages/livebirths/bulletins/birthsummarytablesenglandandwales/2022refreshedpopulations.
19. Age UK, 'Paying for Permanent Residential Care: Paying for a Care Home', accessed 18 May 2024, https://www.ageuk.org.uk/information-advice/care/paying-for-care/paying-for-a-care-home/.
20. GOV.UK, 'Pensioners' Incomes Series: Financial Year 2021 to 2022', accessed 18 May 2024, https://www.gov.uk/government/statistics/pensioners-incomes-series-financial-year-2021-to-2022/pensioners-incomes-series-financial-year-2021-to-2022.
21. Government Digital Service, 'Carer's Allowance', 2024, accessed 26 October 2024, https://www.gov.uk/carers-allowance/eligibility.
22. 'Guide to Financial Support for Members', House of Lords, April 2024, accessed 26 October 2024, https://www.parliament.uk/globalassets/documents/lords-finance-office/2024-25/members-guide-april-2024-web-version_final-version.pdf.
23. P. Butler, 'DWP's Unchecked Database Leaves Tens of Thousands of Carers at Risk of Debt', *The Guardian*, 9 May 2024, accessed 26 October 2024, https://www.theguardian.com/society/article/2024/may/09/dwp-unchecked-database-leaves-tens-thousands-carers-risk-debt.
24. P. Butler, 'Carer's Allowance Scandal Is Not Going Away – but Will DWP Reform Happen?', *The Guardian*, 9 May 2024, accessed 26 October 2024, https://www.theguardian.com/society/article/2024/may/09/carers-allowance-scandal-is-not-going-away-but-will-dwp-reform-happen.
25. P. Butler and J. Halliday, 'National Audit Office to Investigate Growing Scandal over Carer's Allowance', *The Guardian*, 23 May 2024, accessed 26 October 2024, https://www.theguardian.com/society/article/2024/may/23/national-audit-office-to-investigate-growing-scandal-over-carers-allowance.
26. J. Halliday, '"It Feels like Contempt": DWP Tells 85-Year-Old Dementia Patient to Repay £13k', *The Guardian*, 27 May 2024, accessed 26 October 2024, https://www.theguardian.com/society/article/2024/may/27/it-feels-like-contempt-dwp-asks-85-year-old-dementia-patient-to-repay-13k.
27. P. Butler and J. Halliday, 'Ministers Apologise and Return £7,000 in Benefits to Woman, 93, with Dementia', *The Guardian*, 15 May 2024, accessed

26 October 2024, https://www.theguardian.com/society/article/2024/may/15/ministers-apologise-and-return-7000-in-benefits-to-woman-93-with-dementia.
28   E. Johnson and E. Spring, 'The Activity Trap', Activity Alliance, 10 August 2018, accessed 26 October 2024, http://www.activityalliance.org.uk/assets/000/002/433/Activity_Alliance_-_The_Activity_Trap_full_report_Accessible_PDF_FINAL_original.pdf?1538668349; Activity Alliance and IFF Research, 'Annual Disability and Activity Survey 2019/20', Activity Alliance, 28 January 2020, accessed 26 October 2024, http://www.activityalliance.org.uk/assets/000/003/311/Annual_Disability_and_Activity_Survey_%E2%80%93_full_research_report_original.pdf; E. Johnson and D. Nettle, 'Fairness, Generosity and Conditionality in the Welfare System: The Case of UK Disability Benefits', *Global Discourse*, 2020, https://doi.org/10.1332/204378920X15989751152011; E. Johnson and D. Nettle, 'Building on Foundations of Evidence and Intuition: A Reply to Commentaries on "Fairness, Generosity and Conditionality in the Welfare System: The Case of UK Disability Benefits" by Elliot Johnson and Daniel Nettle', *Global Discourse* 13, no. 2 (26 July 2022): 1–8, https://doi.org/10.1332/204378921X16654565200374.
29   E. Johnson, H. Reed and M.T. Johnson, 'Rishi Sunak Wants to Cut the Cost of "Sicknote" Britain. But We've Found a Strong Economic Case for Benefits', *The Conversation*, 24 April 2024, accessed 26 October 2024, http://theconversation.com/rishi-sunak-wants-to-cut-the-cost-of-sicknote-britain-but-weve-found-a-strong-economic-case-for-benefits-228561.
30   Johnson et al, 'Rishi Sunak'.
31   Department for Work and Pensions, 'Family Resources Survey 2022/23: Disability Data Tables', 21 March 2024, accessed 26 October 2024, https://www.gov.uk/government/statistics/family-resources-survey-financial-year-2022-to-2023.
32   Office for National Statistics, 'Age (b), Sex and Unpaid Care', Census 2021, 28 March 2023, accessed 26 October 2024, https://www.ons.gov.uk/datasets/create/filter-outputs/2b1de5bd-1393-4194-8851-dbf2fce8047e#get-data.
33   Common Sense Policy Group, *Act Now*.
34   Howard et al, 'Designing Basic Income Pilots for Community Development'.
35   Government Digital Service, 'Pension Credit', GOV.UK, accessed 28 May 2024, https://www.gov.uk/pension-credit/what-youll-get.
36   Accessed 26 October 2024, https://www.gov.wales/basic-income-care-leavers-wales-pilot-evaluation-annual-report-2023-2024.

# Chapter 6

1   H. Reed, M. Johnson, S. Lansley, E. Johnson, G. Stark and K. Pickett, 'Universal Basic Income is Affordable and Feasible: Evidence from UK Economic Microsimulation Modelling', *The Journal of Poverty and Social Justice* 31, no. 1 (2022): 146–162, https://doi.org/10.1332/175982721X16702368352393.

## Notes

2   D. Summers, 'David Cameron Warns of "New Age of Austerity"', *The Guardian*, 26 April 2009, accessed 27 October 2024, https://www.theguardian.com/politics/2009/apr/26/david-cameron-conservative-economic-policy1.

3   A. Coote, 'Cutting It: The "Big Society" and the New Austerity', NEF, 2010, accessed 27 October 2024, https://neweconomics.org/uploads/files/fe562b1ef767dac0af_g0m6iykyd.pdf.

4   A. Williams, M. Goodwin and P. Cloke, 'Neoliberalism, Big Society, and Progressive Localism', *Environment and Planning A: Economy and Space* 46, no. 12 (2014): 2798–2815, accessed 18 May 2024, https://doi.org/10.1068/a130119p.

5   D. Goodley and K. Runswick-Cole, 'Big Society? Disabled People with the Label of Learning Disabilities and the Queer(y)ing of Civil Society', *Scandinavian Journal of Disability Research* 17, no. 1 (1 August 2015): 1–13, https://doi.org/10.1080/15017419.2014.941924.

6   R. Levitas, 'The Just's Umbrella: Austerity and the Big Society in Coalition Policy and Beyond', *Critical Social Policy* 32, no. 3 (2012): 320–342, accessed 18 May 2024, https://doi.org/10.1177/0261018312444408.

7   A.R. Guinness, 'International Trade and the Making of Peace', *International Affairs* 20, no. 4 (1 October 1944): 495–508, https://doi.org/10.2307/3017130.

8   M.A. Malli, L. Sams, R. Forrester-Jones, G. Murphy and M. Henwood, 'Austerity and the Lives of People with Learning Disabilities: A Thematic Synthesis of Current Literature', *Disability & Society* 33, no. 9 (21 October 2018): 1412–1435, https://doi.org/10.1080/09687599.2018.1497950.

9   K. Poinasamy, *The True Cost of Austerity and Inequality* (London: Oxfam, 2013).

10  O. Jones, *Chavs* (London: Verso, 2011).

11  Standing, *The Precariat*.

12  GOV.UK, 'State of the Nation Report on Social Mobility in Great Britain', accessed 18 May 2024, https://www.gov.uk/government/news/state-of-the-nation-report-on-social-mobility-in-great-britain; Social Mobility Commission, 'State of the Nation 2021: Social Mobility and the Pandemic', HMSO, July 2021, accessed 27 October 2024, https://www.gov.uk/government/publications/state-of-the-nation-2021-social-mobility-and-the-pandemic.

13  S.W. Mintz, 'The Changing Roles of Food in the Study of Consumption', in *Consumption and the World of Goods*, eds. J. Brewer and R. Porter (London: Routledge, 1994), 266–279.

14  W.D. Smith, 'Complications of the Commonplace: Tea, Sugar, and Imperialism', *The Journal of Interdisciplinary History* 23, no. 2 (1992): 259–278, https://doi.org/10.2307/205276.

15  *Father Ted – Mrs. Doyle Fight Scene*, 2009, accessed 27 October 2024, https://www.youtube.com/watch?v=571YIyOkAEM.

16  M. Mauss, *The Gift* (London: Routledge, 2002), 53.

17. M.T. Johnson, 'Rebuilding Authority in "Lumpen" Communities: The Need for Basic Income to Foster Entitlement', *Open Cultural Studies* 7, no. 1 (1 January 2023), https://doi.org/10.1515/culture-2022-0190.
18. 'The English Peasant/Northumbriam Hinds and Ceviot Shepherds', Wikisource, the Free Online Library, accessed 27 May 2024, https://en.wikisource.org/wiki/The_English_Peasant/Northumbriam_Hinds_and_Ceviot_Shepherds.
19. S. Webb, *The Story of the Durham Miners* (London: The Fabian Society, 1921).
20. M. Prasad, S.G. Hoffman and K. Bezila, 'Walking the Line: The White Working Class and the Economic Consequences of Morality', *Politics & Society*, 44, no. 2 (2016), accessed 18 May 2024, https://doi.org/10.1177/0032329216638062.
21. S. O'Connell, *Credit and Community* (Oxford: Oxford University Press, 2009), 1–2.
22. NEF, *Framing the Economy* (London: NEF, 2013).
23. K. Hayward and M. Yar, 'The "Chav" Phenomenon: Consumption, Media and the Construction of a New Underclass', *Crime, Media, Culture* 2, no. 1 (2006): 9–28, accessed 18 May 2024, https://doi.org/10.1177/1741659006061708.
24. Johnson, 'Rebuilding Authority in "Lumpen" Communities'.
25. M. Rustin, 'From the Beginning to the End of Neo-Liberalism in Britain', *OpenDemocracy*, accessed 18 May 2024, https://www.opendemocracy.net/en/opendemocracyuk/after-neo-liberalism-in-britain/.
26. D. Matthews, 'The Working-Class Struggle for Welfare in Britain', *Monthly Review*, 1 February 2018, accessed 27 October 2024, https://monthlyreview.org/2018/02/01/the-working-class-struggle-for-welfare-in-britain/.
27. Johnson et al, 'Exploring the Health Case for Universal Basic Income'.
28. M. Johnson, 'Why Tradespeople, Small Business Owners and the Self-Employed Can Benefit from UBI', *UBI Lab Network*, 29 July 2020, accessed 27 October 2024, https://www.ubilabnetwork.org/blog/why-tradespeople-small-business-owners-and-the-self-employed-can-benefit-from-ubi.
29. A. Chakelian, 'Is Universal Basic Income Possible Here?', *New Statesman*, accessed 25 May 2024, https://www.newstatesman.com/the-weekend-report/2023/07/ubi-possible-britain.

## Chapter 7

1. S. Jeffries, '*Free and Equal* by Daniel Chandler Review – the Road to Fairness', *The Guardian*, 14 April 2023, accessed 27 October 2024, https://www.theguardian.com/books/2023/apr/14/free-and-equal-by-daniel-chandler-review-the-road-to-fairness; D. Chandler, *Free and Equal: What Would a Fair Society Look Like?* (London: Allen Lane, 2023).
2. M.T. Johnson, E.A. Johnson, H. Reed and D. Nettles, 'Can the "Downward Spiral" of Material Conditions, Mental Health and Faith in Government Be Stopped? Evidence from Surveys in "Red Wall" Constituencies', *The British Journal of Politics and International Relations*, 26, no. 1 (2024): 131–148, https://doi.org/10.1177/13691481221146886.

## Notes

3   F. Roosma and W. van Oorschot, 'Public Opinion on Basic Income: Mapping European Support for a Radical Alternative for Welfare Provision', *Journal of European Social Policy*, 30, no. 2 (2020): 190–205, https://doi.org/10.1177/0958928719882827.

4   C. Shoben, 'New Poll: Public Strongly Backing Public Ownership of Energy and Key Utilities', Survation, 15 August 2022, accessed 16 May 2024, https://www.survation.com/new-poll-public-strongly-backing-public-ownership-of-energy-and-key-utilities/.

5   M. Johnson, E. Johnson and D. Nettle, 'Are "Red Wall" Constituencies Really Opposed to Progressive Policy? Examining the Impact of Materialist Narratives for Universal Basic Income', *British Politics* 18 (18 October 2022): 104–127, https://doi.org/10.1057/s41293-022-00220-z.

6   Nettle et al, 'Why Has the COVID-19 Pandemic Increased Support for Universal Basic Income?'.

7   Nettle et al, 'What Do People Want from a Welfare System?'.

8   Nettle et al, 'Why Has the COVID-19 Pandemic Increased Support for Universal Basic Income?'.

9   K.J. Hansen, 'Who Cares If They Need Help? The Deservingness Heuristic, Humanitarianism, and Welfare Opinions', *Political Psychology* 40, no. 2 (2019): 413–430, https://doi.org/10.1111/pops.12506; C. Jensen and M.B. Petersen, 'The Deservingness Heuristic and the Politics of Health Care', *American Journal of Political Science* 61, no. 1 (2017): 68–83, accessed 16 May 2024, https://doi.org/10.1111/ajps.12251.

10  Johnson and Nettle, 'Building on Foundations of Evidence and Intuition'; Johnson and Nettle, 'Fairness, Generosity and Conditionality in the Welfare System'.

11  H. Mercier and D. Sperber, 'Why Do Humans Reason? Arguments for an Argumentative Theory', *Behavioral and Brain Sciences* 34, no. 2 (April 2011): 57–74, https://doi.org/10.1017/S0140525X10000968.

12  Daniel Nettle, *Hanging on to the Edges: Essays on Science, Society and the Academic Life* (Cambridge: Open Book Publishers, 2018), 163–180, https://doi.org/10.11647/obp.0155.

13  Van Parijs and Vanderborght, *Basic Income*; P. Van Parijs, 'Basic Income: A Simple and Powerful Idea for the Twenty-First Century', *Politics & Society* 32, no. 1 (March 2004): 7–39, https://doi.org/10.1177/0032329203261095; Chandler, *Free and Equal: What Would a Fair Society Look Like?*; Pettit, *Just Freedom*.

14  'The Overton Window', Mackinac Center, accessed 16 May 2024, https://www.mackinac.org/OvertonWindow.

15  E.A. Johnson, I. Hardill, M.T. Johnson and D. Nettle, 'Breaking the Overton Window: On the Need for Adversarial Co-Production', *Evidence & Policy* 20, no. 3 (2024): 393–405, https://doi.org/10.1332/17442648 Y2023D000000005; H. Mercier and H. Landemore, 'Reasoning Is for Arguing: Understanding the Successes and Failures of Deliberation', *Political Psychology* 33, no. 2 (2012): 243–258, https://doi.org/10.1111/j.1467-9221.2012.00873.x.

[16] 'Towards the Manifestos: What's the Agenda for Fixing Poverty and Tackling Inequality?', accessed 26 May 2024, https://www.kcl.ac.uk/policy-institute/assets/towards-the-manifestos-solutions-for-tackling-poverty-and-inequality-full-report.pdf.

## Conclusion

[1] T. Helm, 'Brexit Has Completely Failed for UK, Say Clear Majority of Britons – Poll', *The Observer*, 30 December 2023, accessed 27 October 2024, https://www.theguardian.com/politics/2023/dec/30/britons-brexit-bad-uk-poll-eu-finances-nhs.
[2] See https://basicincome.org/ for a source of news on the basic income landscape.

# Index

References to figures are in *italics*; references to tables are in **bold**.

**A**
Action for Children (charity) 50
administrative simplicity 14, 21, 98–99, 102, 104
agency 78–83
Alaska Permanent Fund Dividend 26
alcohol consumption 25–26, 54–55
antisocial behaviour 25–26, 52, 64
anxiety *see* stress
argumentative justifications 99–106, 107, 108
austerity 77–79, 81–82
authority to act 78–83, 85

**B**
Bambra, Clare 36, 53
basic income pilots 74–75, 87
*see also* cash transfer trials
basic income schemes
  scheme 1 12–13, **13**, 31–33, 34, 38, 91
  scheme 2 13, **13**, 32, 49, 61, 98
  scheme 3 13, **13**, 32, 33, 38, 49, 61, 98
benefits system *see* welfare system
Beveridge, William 107
Big Local Jarrow (community organisation) 64
Big Society policy 78, 81–82
Birmingham 67
Blair, Tony 36
Blyth, Northumberland 39
Brady, David 52–53
Brazil 36
Brexit 112

Brexit Party voters 94
Buffalo Community Centre, Blyth 39
Bullock, Christopher 48

**C**
carbon tax 13
care 65–75
  care workers 66, 68–69, 73
  childhood care 23–24, 62, 66–69
  positive effect of basic income 23–24, 62, 71–74
  social care 69, 74–75
  unpaid adult care 23–24, 69–71, 72, 73
  welfare payments 65–66, 68, 69–71, 72–73
Carer's Allowance 65, 69–70, 72
Cartie, Eileen 39
CASCADE, Cardiff University 75
cash transfer trials 36–37, 57
  *see also* basic income pilots
centre-left political parties 89–90, 91
  *see also* Labour Party
Chakalian, Anoosh 87
Chandler, Daniel 90
Child Benefit 31, 66–67, 111
children 33, 66, 66–67, 74–75
  *see also* parenting
Children and Families Newcastle 50
Coalition government (2010–2015) 78
*The Cobler of Preston* (Bullock) 48
collection risk 55–56, 57
collective bargaining 89
community life 61–63, 78–83

133

Conservative Party 10–11, 88–89, 112
  *see also* Coalition government
  (2010–2015)
Conservative voters 93–94, *94*, 97–98,
  *97*, 108
Coram Childcare Survey 67
corporate accountancy 24
COVID-19 pandemic 73, 92–93, 95,
  99, 101
crime rates 61, 64

**D**

Darlington, County Durham 87
de Courson, Benoît 60–61
dependency 80–83
deservingness 99
desperation threshold 59–61
disabilities 66
disability-related benefits 10, 71, 83,
  103
distributive effect of basic income
  31–32
domination 46–47
double dividend 54–58, 61–63, 77, 87
drug consumption 25–26

**E**

Eastern Band of Cherokee Indians 57
employment *see* work
entitlement to basic income 14

**F**

Family Resources Survey 68
*Father Ted* (TV comedy) 80
Feeney, Graeme 87
fiscal neutrality 13, *15*
food insecurity 11
Franklin, Benjamin 48
*Free and Equal* (Chandler) 90
freedom 22, 26, 27, 46–47
Friedman, Milton 27, 88
furlough scheme 93, 102, 103

**G**

Germany 36, 68
gig economy 21, 44, 45–46, 48
Gini coefficient 33, 34

government policy 34, 35–36, 45,
  52–53
government provision of services
  21–22
Graeber, David 11
Green Party 107
Green Party voters *94*
*The Guardian* 90, 95

**H**

Hayek, Friedrich 27, 88
health 78–83
  correlation with poverty 34–37
  cost of ill health 3
  life expectancy 9–10, 57
  positive effect of basic income 26,
    37–38, 112–113
  preventative health 54–55
  stress as risk factor 40
  welfare system effects on 83–84
high-income households 31–32, **32**, 49
homeowners 93, *94*
Hugo, Victor 61

**I**

*I, Daniel Blake* (film) 47
income tax 13, 23, 29, 32, 95–98, *97*,
  102, 111
individual responsibility 25–26
inequality levels 33
infant mortality 66
inflation 13

**J**

Jane (Durham health worker) 108–109
Jarrow, South Tyneside 12, 64
Jefferson, Thomas 26
Johnson, Tommy 85, 86
Jones, Owen 79
Joseph Rowntree Foundation 21

**K**

Keynes, John Maynard 10

**L**

Labour Force Survey 68–69
labour market 23, 47–48

# Index

Labour Party  71, 77, 89, 91, 92, 107–108, 112
Labour voters  93–94, *94*, 97–98, *97*
Levelling Up funding  39
*Levelling Up the United Kingdom* (UK government White Paper)  9–10
Levitas, Ruth  78
Liberal Democrat voters  *94*
life expectancy  9–10, 57
London  67
low-income households  31, **32**

## M

Macchia, Lucia  45, 53
Manchester  67
Mauss, Marcel  80
McCartney, Peter  84–85, 86
medical appointments  83–84
medieval serfdom  80–81
mental health  35, 37, 38, 40–41, 66, 112–113
Middlesbrough, North Yorkshire  67
Minimum Income Standard (MIS)  13
*Les Misérables* (Hugo)  61
Moores, John  81
moral arguments  22–28

## N

National Audit Office  70
National Health Service (NHS)  13, 28
  *see also* health
National Insurance  13
neoliberal reforms  10–11, 77–79, 81–82
Newcastle upon Tyne  50–51
Noden, Sally  50
Norway  92
nursery costs  67–68

## O

O'Connell, Sean  81
Oswald, Andrew  45, 53
Overton window  106–108

## P

parenting
  birth rates  69
  childcare costs  67–68
  positive effect of basic income 23–24, 62, 72
  poverty rates  33, 66–67
parenting (continued)
  single parents  68–69, 72
  welfare payments  65–66, 68
participation income  25
Pension Credit  72–73
Pepper, Gillian  17, 54
Pettit, Philip  47
popular immiseration  11
positive effects of basic income
  overview  14–18, *15*
  improvements for communities 61–63, 78–83
  improvements in care  23–24, 62, 71–74
  improvements in health  37–38, 112–113
  lower crime rates  61, 64
  reduced poverty  30–33, **32**, 37–38, 39
  simplified administration  98–99, 102, 104
  work-related advantages  84–86, 87
poverty  29–39
  child poverty  33, 66–67
  correlation with health  34–37
  effect on risk taking  59–61
  focus on short-term  54–56
  immorality of  27
  impact of public policies  34, 35–36, 39, 52–53
  importance of reducing  33–37
  main determinant of  34
  positive effect of basic income 30–33, **32**, 37–38, 39
  poverty line  29, 33, 34, 68
  prevalence of  11, 34
  whilst in paid employment  21
precarity  44, 83
  *see also* uncertainty
Pregnant Then Screwed (charity)  68
public opinion  90–109
  argumentative justifications  99, 106, 107, 108
  costs versus benefit trade-off  95–98, *97*

public opinion (continued)
   European study  92
   Overton window  106–108
   Red Wall constituencies  90–91, 93–95, *94*, 101–106
   relevant considerations  98–99
public service provision  21–22

## R

Rawls, John  59
Red Wall constituencies  90–91, 93–95, *94*, 101–106
Resolution Foundation (think tank)  66–67
risk taking  58–61, 85, 86
Russell, Roweena  64

## S

Scandinavia  36
short-term perspectives  52, 53, 54–58, 64
smoking  54–55
social care  69, 74–75
social legacy  24–25
Standing, Guy  2, 44, 62, 79
stress  40–51
   as concept  41–43
   exacerbated by welfare system  45–48
   physiological reactions  41, 42–43
   positive effect of basic income  48–50, 76–77
   prevalence of  40
   public opinion on  27–28, 98–99
   relation to health  40
   role of uncertainty  41–44, 48, 50–51
Sweden  68, 92
Switzerland  92

## T

tax avoidance  24
taxation  13, 23, 29, 32, 95–98, *97*, 102, 111
terminology  14
Thatcherism  10–11
time horizons (individuals)  52, 53, 54–58

*The Times*  39
tradespeople  84–85, 86, 87
Turchin, Peter  11

## U

UK Household Longitudinal Study  37–38
uncertainty
   link with stress  41–44, 48, 50–51
   positive effect of basic income  48–50
   in welfare system  45–48
Understanding Society survey  37–38
United States  36
universal basic income  14, 101
Universal Credit  18–19, 20, 21, 31, 39, 45–46, 48, 65, 67, 68, 70, 72, 102, 103–104

## V

van Parijs, Philippe  2
Vanderborght, Yannick  2

## W

Wales  105
wealth taxes  13
welfare state  82, 91, 107
welfare system
   basic income payments compared  31
   big government approach  77–78
   conditionality of  14, 18–20, 45–48
   cost of  10, 19, 104, 110–111
   designed for earlier decades  20–21, 49
   as disincentive to work  19–20, 45–46, 103
   experiences of  28
   fraud and error  104
   impact on GPs  83–84
   inefficiencies of  12, 103–104
   perverse incentives in  19–20, 65–66
   uncertainties of  45–48, 103–104
   *see also* Carer's Allowance; disability-related benefits; government policy; Pension Credit; Universal Credit

window of discourse 106–108
Woolf, Virginia 3
work
    collective bargaining 89
    economic inactivity 10
    positive effect of basic income 84–86, 87
    price work 84, 86
    relationship with 108
    uncertainties of 44, 48, 83
    *see also* labour market

**Y**

young people
    care leavers basic income trial 74–75
    perceptions of 27–28, 57, 79
    stifling of contribution 86
    support for basic income 93, *94*

**Z**

zero-hours contracts 44, 48

www.ingramcontent.com/pod-product-compliance
Lightning Source LLC
Chambersburg PA
CBHW031155020426
42333CB00013B/679